ADHD

The Essential Guide

Diane
Paul

ADHD – The Essential Guide is also available in accessible formats for people with any degree of visual impairment. The large print edition and eBook (with accessibility features enabled) are available from Need2Know. Please let us know if there are any special features you require and we will do our best to accommodate your needs.

First published in Great Britain in 2012 by
Need2Know
Remus House
Coltsfoot Drive
Peterborough
PE2 9BF
Telephone 01733 898103
Fax 01733 313524
www.need2knowbooks.co.uk

Contents

Introduction

It isn't much fun living with a child who has attention deficit disorder (ADD) and even less fun if your child has attention deficit hyperactivity disorder (ADHD). For a start, most people think they're just attention-seeking or, even worse, badly brought up. 'It's the parents' fault,' they say. 'They don't know how to bring up children.'

To be accused of poor parenting when you spend all your time chasing around after an unruly youngster who is disruptive at home and at school is the last straw, but you'll be pleased to know that your parenting has nothing to do with your child's behavioural difficulties, clumsiness, impulsiveness or poor planning ability. Neither are they suffering from brain damage, as the name 'minimal brain dysfunction' led parents to believe in the 1960s. Neural wiring in the brain tends to be different for children with ADHD, resulting in some of the more extreme forms of behaviour outlined in this book, and not all children will display all of the symptoms associated with it.

Many of these cases go undiagnosed, sometimes for years, and during that time your child may have been excluded from school several times, missing part of their education and becoming isolated from their peers. This can have severe repercussions on their future in general and the chance of a fulfilling career and social life. ADHD will follow them into adulthood and many adults have ADHD without knowing it.

That's why it's so important to understand the nature of ADHD in your child's early years, to know what symptoms to look out for and where to go for help, advice and assessments. The earlier your child is diagnosed, the better.

This book aims to bring together the information you need to help your child through the tangle of legislation and the lengthy processes available to assess and treat their condition, so that they can integrate into society and enjoy a more fulfilling life.

How can you tell if your child has ADHD or if they are just being generally boisterous? I've provided a checklist of possible symptoms, which should give a fair indication. Each chapter also contains advice on how systems work, who to contact and the sort of response you can expect.

What sort of treatment will they have and who will diagnose them? Do drugs help or are they dangerous? What sort of side effects could your child experience by taking them? Are there other forms of treatment that would help? Should you change their diet? All these questions and many more are answered in this book.

It isn't plain sailing though. Getting assessments isn't that easy and the Department of Health has been accused of operating a postcode lottery.

Doors were firmly closed to an outsider in the ADHD world; emails and phone messages went ignored, as did postings on campaign websites and requests for information packs that never arrived. I soon realised I was on my own, apart from several parents who were prepared to tell me their stories. Only lack of space prevents me from retelling them in this book but my thanks to them for taking the time to contact me. Their input was enlightening. I even faced hostility and anger from the co-ordinator of a support group who demanded to know what right I had to write a book about ADHD. I had no idea there might be a law against it.

How essential then, is it to collect together the mass of information that exists and pull it together into a guide for parents faced with similar reactions? I knew then that I had to continue.

Why does your child have ADHD? Nobody seems to have an answer to that. Research has thrown up a variety of reasons, all of which are covered in the book. As is usual, researchers may disagree with one another and not enough is known yet about ADHD to give a definite reason. However, they are all worth considering so I have included them. I have tried to write impartially and present all sides of the issue.

The role of the parents and the family are crucial to supporting children with ADHD, so the more you understand about the condition, the better it will be all round. If parents can work with teachers in bringing about a better quality of life for the child, everyone will benefit, including the other kids at school.

Nobody said it was going to be a doddle but with vital information to hand and the right kind of support, parents can move forward with the knowledge they need to improve the quality of life for themselves, their families and their child. ADHD can't be cured, but it can be controlled. Information is also provided for teachers and carers working with children suffering from ADHD.

I would like to thank Manchester nutritional therapist Clare Jones for reading my chapter on nutrition and making some factual corrections and practical suggestions to improve the content, for which I am more than grateful.

My thanks also to Eleanor at NHS Quality Improvement Scotland for her patience in explaining the roles of SIGN and the Scottish Medicines Consortium, and for sending me the information so promptly.

Special thanks to Andrea Bilbow from ADDISS for all her helpful advice and comments, which enabled me to make additions and corrections to this second edition.

Special thanks to Cathy Stigley from Alaska and Brighton, Regional Education Director of Europe for The HANDLE Institute, and Suzie Gorringe from Tonbridge, Kent, a HANDLE Screener (and Practitioner Intern). Cathy and Suzie both enlightened me about the work of HANDLE and its non-drug treatment of people of all ages with learning, behaviour and development issues, including ADD/ADHD.

Disclaimer

This book is for general information on ADHD. It is not intended to replace professional medical advice. It can be used alongside professional medical advice, but you are strongly advised to consult your health-care professional.

Definitions

It is easy for the symptoms of people with ADD/ADHD to be confused with the symptoms of those displayed in the following disorders and some of them co-exist (referred to as co-morbidity).

Asperger's Syndrome	A neurobiological disorder, similar to autism, with normal IQ and hypersensitivity. Some are highly talented. Often incorrectly diagnosed with ADD/ADHD.
Attention Deficit Disorder (ADD)	Similar to ADHD but without the hyperactivity. Usually lumped together: ADD/ADHD.
Autistic Spectrum Disorder (ASD) (Autism and Asperger's Syndrome)	A fairly new term denoting sub-groups to autism. Difficulties with verbal/non-verbal communication; poor interactions with others; repetitive, obsessive or restricted behaviours.
Bipolar Affective Disorder Bipolar I = Hypomania Bipolar II = Hypomania + Depression	Also termed manic depression. Mood swings in varying degrees. Hypomania displays over-confidence and elation.
Conduct Behaviour Disorder	Repeated aggressive behaviour towards others, their property or animals. More severe type of ODD (see opposite page.).
Delirium	Confused state of brain function; includes hyperactivity, poor concentration, disorganised thinking, sleep and memory problems.
Dyslexia	Specific learning difficulty involving reading, writing and spelling. Neurological basis: unusual brain wiring.

Dyspraxia	Neurological disorder involving motor co-ordination; hard to plan and execute movement/tasks. Clumsy children. ADHD often co-exists.
Emotionally Unstable Personality Disorder	Impulsive: symptoms include impulsive behaviour and violence when criticised. Borderline: impulsive, unstable relationships, needs are unrealistic.
Epilepsy (Seizure Disorder)	Sudden changes in brain function cause seizures involving fainting, trembling or unconsciousness.
Hyperkinetic Disorder (HKD)	A sub-type of ADHD. Language and motor delays, antisocial conduct. Most are undiagnosed.
Language Disorder	Communication difficulty, especially in understanding language, finding words and using them.
Obsessive-Compulsive Disorder (OCD)	Anxiety disorder characterised by excessive worrying about their life situation; frightening thoughts and images; sufferer carries out ritualised actions to protect themselves.
Oppositional Defiant Disorder (ODD)	Negative, hostile and aggressive behaviour to adults and peers. Mood swings, frustration, swearing, alcohol and/or substance abuse, poor self-esteem.
Sleep Apnoea	Air flow to the lungs is stopped during sleep, causing the sleeper to wake up in order to breathe again. Causes sleep deprivation.
Tourette's Syndrome	Inherited neurological condition causing uncontrollable tics, sudden movements and calling out inappropriate comments or swearing. Symptoms can include OCD, ADD, depression, anxiety, self-harming.

Chapter One

What is ADHD?

ADHD, like dyslexia in the past, has been slow to gain recognition from educational and medical authorities, some of whom still believe that there is no such thing and that children with ADHD are just badly behaved or the product of poor parenting. It isn't uncommon for doctors to tell parents that their child's unorthodox behaviour is due to problems at home, mixing with the wrong children, the 'terrible twos or threes' or not enough exercise.

How does it show up?

Most young children can be full of energy and bounce, and as they grow older it's quite normal for them to assert their authority and have the odd tantrum. But if your child is showing signs of consistent and repetitive negative behaviour, it may be time to take a closer look.

ADHD is particularly hard to pinpoint because the symptoms may be just part of the child's normal development and some of the symptoms can mimic or occur in other disorders or co-exist with them. They don't all follow the same patterns. So what makes ADHD behaviour so different?

ADHD is a biological condition caused by an imbalance of the chemicals in the brain's neurotransmitter. It occurs in the frontal lobes of the brain where decisions are made to check impulsive behaviour and self-monitoring. It is hereditary and long term, so about half of those affected will continue to display symptoms as adolescents and adults, albeit in a modified form. Three main types of behaviour have been noted:

- Overactive and impulsive (hyperactive).

- Inattentive (ADD types).

- Both types combined (this is the majority of cases).

'ADHD is particularly hard to pinpoint because the symptoms may be just part of the child's normal development and some of them can mimic or occur in other disorders or co-exist with them.'

How many people have ADHD?

This is a hard one to guesstimate. Not all cases of ADHD are officially recognised and you might find yourself being given a variety of differing statistics. They could be anything from 1-20%, depending on the parameters used by researchers in different countries and which of the two main diagnostic criteria are used – DSM-IV (3-5%) or ICD-10 (about 0.5%). (See chapter 2 for more information on this.)

More facts and figures can be found in *Understanding ADHD – A Parent's Guide to Attention Deficit Hyperactivity Disorder in Children* by C. Green and K. Chee, *All About ADHD* by Dr Jo Borrill, the Mental Health Foundation (see the book list), the ADDISS website (see the help list) and NICE guidelines for children and adolescents with ADHD, their families, carers and the public (see the further information section in the help list).

'It seems to be on the rise, probably because it is becoming more recognised.'

Some of these facts appear below.

Frequently quoted facts and figures

▪ Mental Health Foundation figures indicate that ADHD affects from 0.5-2% of schoolchildren in the UK. NHS Direct places that at between 3-9%. These figures, and others, may be based on different criteria, showing how difficult it is to arrive at an accurate figure.

▪ In the USA, figures are estimated to be about 9% of eight to 15-year-olds (2.4 million).

▪ The generally quoted figure worldwide is around 5%.

▪ It seems to be on the rise, probably because it is becoming more recognised.

▪ Previously, children were punished for disruptive behaviour.

▪ It is generally noted around the age of five.

▪ Four to five times more boys than girls have it.

▪ Girls are less likely to be diagnosed than boys.

- Some studies compare figures in different countries or areas. Three times more Chinese than English boys are said to have ADHD, for example.

- It is thought that children from poorer environments are more likely to develop it.

- About 50% of children with ADHD display specific learning difficulties, like dyspraxia or dyslexia.

- They can have many more disorders, among them conduct behaviour disorder and oppositional defiant disorder, anxiety, depression and low self-esteem. (See Definitions.)

- ADHD has no bearing on intelligence.

- As many as 80% may become ADHD adolescents.

- About 60% may still show ADHD symptoms as adults.

- Only about 10% of ADHD children are getting help.

- The majority of ADHD children are undiagnosed.

Will role models help?

If a child has ADHD it doesn't signify that they will become one of life's misfits. But it seems to be the fashion these days to 'out' a string of celebrities, past and present, who succeeded in life despite their childhood handicaps. Google will provide you with dozens of long lists of the famous, whose originators claim that they displayed ADHD symptoms in childhood but are unable to produce a shred of evidence to support their theories.

When we find it so hard to identify today's children with ADHD, I'm not sure how anyone could know for sure whether Leonardo Da Vinci, Albert Einstein or Christopher Columbus had it just from reading about them, and even though Mozart did seem to be hyperactive, we can't possibly know why.

'The majority of ADHD children are undiagnosed.'

Gifted children

It is possible that many of these people were famous because they were gifted; gifted children being among those who are often overlooked in education. They can feel held back and become frustrated, showing some of the same behavioural problems as those on our lists. This may account for the current trend to assume that they had dyslexia or ADHD, when in fact their energy was fuelled by their urge to create the next project taking shape in their minds, often before they'd finished their previous one. Gifted children can be highly sensitive, very energetic, can become bored easily, and inattentive. They can challenge authority and become frustrated and fidgety if they lose interest. They can also be withdrawn and have difficulty expressing their feelings. Sound familiar? Gifted children may also have ADHD. Underperforming at school may put them on the average level, which may satisfy teachers and parents, so both ADHD and giftedness may be overlooked.

According to Professor Michael Fitzgerald, Henry Marsh Professor of Child and Adolescent Psychiatry at Trinity College, Dublin, Lord Byron, Oscar Wilde and singer Kurt Cobain may have had ADHD. Professor Fitzgerald's research studied a variety of high achievers, including Che Guevara and Pablo Picasso and concluded that the same genes were linked to risk-taking. While some ADHD people are led into crime, others achieve in art, science and exploration, releasing their untapped potential.

Fitzgerald says, 'People with ADHD have symptoms of inattentiveness, but they often also have a capacity to hyper-focus on a narrow area that is of particular interest to them. Clearly ADHD is not a guarantee of genius, but the focused work rate that it produces may enable creative genius to flourish. For example, Kurt Cobain – who we know was prescribed the anti-hyperactivity drug Ritalin as a child – had an amazing ability to focus on writing music.'

At the annual meeting of the Royal College of Psychiatrists' Faculty of Academic Psychiatry in 2010, Fitzgerald suggested that Lord Byron may have had ADHD. 'He had a turbulent life, at school he was often in trouble and as an adult he engaged in criminal activities and was eventually forced to flee the country. But he was also the greatest lyric poet in the English language.' Sir Walter Raleigh was quite reckless. 'His insatiable quest for new stimulation and risk-taking behaviour also made him a famous soldier, adventurer and explorer.'

Living role models

Among the living on the lists is American actor Robin Williams who is a fast talker and shows bags of energy in his TV interviews, but I have never seen confirmation that he has ADHD; we could say the same of comedian Lenny Henry, but his name isn't on the lists.

As a journalist, I've interviewed many celebrities and generally find that they have rather different personalities to those they display under the public gaze, so perhaps we shouldn't judge them from their performances. It's no surprise to find the same names popping up in lists of other conditions, such as dyslexia and left-handedness.

Some more famous names:

- Tom Cruise
- Napoleon
- Steven Spielberg
- Sylvester Stallone
- Vincent Van Gogh
- Stevie Wonder
- Bill Gates
- Susan Hampshire
- Stephen Hawking
- Dustin Hoffman

Names taken from a list compiled by the late Kitty Petty. Visit www.kpinst.org/famous.html.

Although it's great to think that such prominent people succeeded in spite of their traits, it's unfair to give children a false boost to their morale when we have no proof. Many people suffer from some of the symptoms like anxiety and depression, particularly creative people, but that doesn't mean they have ADHD.

However, singer Daniel Bedingfield has openly stated in media interviews that not only does he have dyslexia but at 15 he was diagnosed as hyperactive and that his life changed when he began taking Ritalin three years later. At this point he began to like himself and he learned how to control his energy, some of which has been channelled into his songwriting.

Jack Osbourne, son of Ozzie, hated school and was diagnosed with dyslexia aged eight, and ADHD aged 10. 'Pray hard and you will get better' was apparently the reaction of his school in Los Angeles. He changed to a special needs school and was prescribed Ritalin.

Roger Graef, criminologist, broadcaster and film producer, discovered he had mild ADHD when he heard a talk about young offenders and ADHD given by a policeman at the Sheffield International Documentary Festival. Graef identified with 12 of the 20 symptoms mentioned in chapter 1. As a result, he became a patron of ADDISS, the ADHD charity. In a 'coming out' article he wrote in *The Daily Mail* in 2007, he stated, 'But my experience is different. It's been a gift – albeit with unpleasant side effects, especially for others. No one ever talks about the good side of ADHD.'

On the upside, he cites:

- Being able to do three things at once.

- Listening to the radio, writing and taking phone calls – on different topics.

- Needing little sleep but having bags of energy.

- Giving talks without notes and ending on time.

- Grasping the point fast and seeing possibilities where others see problems.

Graef's excessive energy has allowed him to direct 26 plays, two operas, two TV dramas and over 130 documentary films and studio dramas. He has worked as a director, producer, series producer and executive producer. He has written three books and many articles, gives talks and serves on boards and committees. ADHD has affected his personal life but he says he has 'come to terms with some of ADHD's more destructive features.'

'So I hope the parents and teachers of children with these problems, and those who have suffered from ADHD, will see beyond its drawbacks to a future of excitement and creativity if sufferers are given the chance to learn how to use their energy positively.'

Filmmaker Roger Graef, *The Daily Mail*, 10th September 2007.

Impressionist Rory Bremner talked about his ADHD 'tendencies' in a BBC Radio 4 documentary he presented on adult ADHD. Bremner has not been officially diagnosed but suspected he had ADHD four years ago when a young relative, who was diagnosed with the condition, displayed similar symptoms.

Bremner related his forgetfulness, lack of organisation, impulsiveness and inability to concentrate back to his childhood. He said he has difficulty sitting still, his mind wanders and he has no common sense. In the programme, *ADHD and Me*, Professor Eric Taylor, an expert on ADHD from King's College, London commented that some of Bremner's tendencies suggested ADHD. Bremner now has a better understanding of the condition and how society's attitude towards ADHD needs to change.

A support group for adults with ADHD was set up at St Catherine's Hospital, Liverpool and there, Rory Bremner met group member Gary and talked to him. The programme can be heard on BBC iPlayer,

http://www.bbc.co.uk/iplayer/episode/b011c0nn/ADHD_and_Me/

Singer Sting's partner, Trudie Styler, a mother of four, is hugely successful in her own right as an actor, filmmaker, eco-activist and UNICEF ambassador. She went to school in the Midlands in the 1960s and was labelled 'backwards' because she had reading difficulties. She also has dyslexia, which is not uncommon with ADHD. She continued to struggle with her later schooling and it was her religious faith that carried her through. Acting as another character helped her distance herself from the real Trudie.

Many of Sting and Styler's extended family have ADHD and dyslexia. She relies heavily on her PA to keep her organised but the condition has helped her understand other people and how to communicate with them. Yoga also helps to give her strength and meditation stills her mind and helps her focus. Sometimes she takes the drug Adderall to help script reading. In an article in the Huffington Post, USA, in May 2011, she said, 'Celebrate who you intrinsically are, listen for the small voice. Instead of buying into "I just can't do it", reach out and ask for help.'

'I have had ADHD since I was a child and I still have it ... It has helped my songwriting because when I write songs my brain is flooded with adrenaline and endorphins. All my songs have been influenced by my condition.'

Singer Daniel Bedingfield, *The Record*, January 2005.

History

ADHD may seem like a recently diagnosed phenomenon but some of its characteristics were noted as far back as 1845. However, it has gone through a variety of labels and development since that time.

Key advancements

- 1798 Sir Alexander Crichton, Scottish physician, described a condition with similar symptoms to ADHD in his book, *An Inquiry into the Nature and Origin of Mental Derangement*, in the chapter on Attention. A patient could be born with it or acquire it from a disease and it improved with age. It was described as 'mental restlessness' or 'the fidgets'. He recommended 'special educational intervention'.

- 1845 Dr Heinrich Hoffman (1809-1894), a German physician and writer, is thought to have described this condition. However, he was best known for his children's book, *Shockhead Peter* or *Slovenly Peter*, which gave his view of children's negative behaviour. His miscreants received quite dramatic and gory punishments.

- 1902 Morbid defect of moral control. Recognition of an impulsive disorder studied by paediatrician Sir George Frederic Still (1868-1941) in the UK. His three published lectures for the Royal Society of Medicine described uninhibited under eight-year-olds with negative tendencies such as aggression, defiance and attention deficit. He noted family members with depression, alcohol addiction and behavioural disorders, which suggested a biological basis.

- 1922 Post-encephalitic behaviour disorders.

- 1937 First use of stimulants by Dr Charles Bradley (1902-1979) during observations of children with behavioural problems at what is now Bradley Hospital, Rhode Island. Formerly a children's hospital founded by his great uncle, Bradley was medical director. After prescribing Benzedrine to 30 children, he noted a spectacular improvement among 14 of them after one week, especially with schoolwork. It was 25 years before stimulants were used more widely for ADHD.

- 1956   Ritalin recommended as the best treatment for hyperactivity.

- 1960   Minimal brain dysfunction.

- 1968   Hyperkinetic reaction. Other symptoms noted, including impulsiveness and poor attention span.

- 1973   Paediatric allergist, Benjamin Feingold MD (1899-1982), suggested that artificial colourings, flavourings and preservatives caused hyperactivity in children. His diet, excluding these substances, produced a notable improvement on a wide range of symptoms both physical and behavioural in children. Critics suggested that family involvement and more attention to the child could have been responsible. The debate is ongoing. He produced the books *Why Your Child Is Hyperactive* (1975) and *The Feingold Cookbook for Hyperactive Children* (1979).

- 1980   Attention deficit disorder/attention deficit hyperactivity disorder with two separate diagnoses.

- 1980   Sally Bundy and her mother, Vicky Colquhoun, first linked a lack of essential fatty acids (EFAs) with ADHD. The two women launched the Hyperactive Children's Support Group (HACSG). It took 15 years for their theory to be confirmed by researchers.

- 1987   ADD joined with ADHD, which appeared to include behavioural difficulties.

- 1996   Adderall recommended as a better treatment for ADHD.

- 1999   Concerta and Focalin become recommended treatments.

- 2000   National Institute of Clinical Excellence (NICE) published recommendations on current best practice in the UK in line with the US.

- 2002   The International Consensus Statement from international scientists and those treating ADHD in 12 countries, including the UK and USA, is produced, making practice consistent.

- 2003 Strattera – the first non-stimulant with anti-depressant characteristics used to boost norepinephrine in the brain.

- 2005 Adderall was withdrawn in North America.

- 2008 Today defined as attention deficit hyperactivity disorder.

Action points

- Read books about ADHD and other linked conditions. Borrow or order them from your local library or their inter-library loan scheme; buy them from major bookshops or through www.amazon.co.uk. Search for out-of-print books in second-hand bookshops.

- Surf the Internet for sites relating to ADHD. Do this with caution. There are dozens of websites to choose from and some may contain inaccurate information or mythology. Government websites are most reliable or NHS Direct at www.nhsdirect.nhs.uk. (See the help list for further information.)

- It's a good idea to begin observing your child and noting their behaviour. See if there are patterns to disruptive episodes, like just before teatime or going to bed.

- Contact organisations that issue information packs on ADHD. Some contacts are given at the end of this book.

- Don't forget when writing to people for information to enclose a stamped addressed envelope.

Summing Up

You may suspect from your child's behaviour that they have ADHD but it's hard to be certain. They could be displaying the normal boisterous behaviour of any small child. All children are different; some may be quieter and more reserved than others, and some may be more disruptive. Observing your child and noting their behaviour is the first step. Knowing the characteristics of an ADHD child is crucial, so your quest for knowledge will not only enlighten you but will also enable you to deal with the professionals without being fazed or feeling helpless when they use complex terms or try to blind you with science.

Chapter Two

Signs and Symptoms

Signs to watch out for

As they mature, energetic children usually become less boisterous and calm down. But some of the symptoms displayed by ADHD children are common to other conditions, making it difficult to obtain an accurate diagnosis. In addition, there are other conditions that can co-exist with ADHD and override them. The symptoms can vary from child to child and it depends which of the three types of ADHD your child has. If they are showing more of the characteristics of any of the three categories of behaviour shown in chapter 1, compared to the average child of their age group, then it may be worth investigating.

Once they start school, their symptoms may get worse and their behaviour may begin to affect the other pupils and staff. It also doesn't make any difference how intelligent they are – intelligence isn't a measure of ADHD. If your child has ADD, they won't be so noticeable because they tend to daydream and, although they may not pay attention to what's going on, they aren't disruptive or noisy.

You can carry out your own observations at home before deciding whether it would be best to contact the professionals for a proper diagnosis. Teachers can help by noting characteristics in the classroom.

The table overleaf shows typical symptoms.

'It doesn't make any difference how intelligent they are – intelligence isn't a measure of ADHD.'

Symptoms checklist

Use the tick boxes below to record your observations. This is not intended as a scientific study, nor is it a test for diagnosis, but is merely a simple way of noting down your child's behavioural patterns for your own information. Tests are available but they have to be carried out by professionals using the accepted criteria.

Symptoms	Sometimes	Often	Never
Accident-prone			
Aggression			
Allergic reactions			
Anxiety			
Clumsiness			
Depression			
Disruptiveness			
Dreaminess			
Emotional immaturity			
Fidgety			
Forgetfulness			
Handwriting difficulties			
Hyperactivity			
Impulsiveness			
Inability to complete tasks			
Inattentiveness			
Interrupt conversations			
Irritability			
Lack of concentration			
Language (or speech) difficulties			

Learning difficulties			
Low self-esteem			
Mal-organisation			
Mood swings			
Non-conformity			
Poor co-ordination			
Restlessness			
Sleep disorders			
Specific learning difficulties			
Talkative (overly so)			
Unafraid of danger			
Undetermined handedness			

Symptoms in infants

You may notice some signs of difficult behaviour in your baby or toddler. It may be hard to get them to go to sleep and you may have found yourself pacing up and down with them in your arms to no avail at night. Some babies sleep for a short while, then wake up demanding full attention and nursing for long periods. Even when they do get to sleep, they can have dreadful nightmares.

They can cry and scream to excess, leaving you helpless to know how to calm them down. Some babies are hard to feed and dribble a lot but are very thirsty. They may repeatedly bang their heads against the wall and rock the cot back and forth. Some may begin to walk and run about without going through the crawling stage first.

Symptoms at pre-school

Once they are able to walk and run around, they may do so excessively, falling over and having accidents. They will find it hard to keep still or settle down when stories are read out and they may attack other children, hitting, spitting and scratching them. They don't care if they get punished and have no fear of teachers or people in authority. This behaviour is likely to follow them into primary school, where further symptoms may develop.

Diagnostic criteria

Health professionals have a choice of two international sets of diagnostic criteria to follow when identifying ADHD.

These are:

'They don't care if they get punished and have no fear of teachers or people in authority.'

- *The Diagnostic and Statistical Manual of Mental Disorders,* 4th edition, referred to as DSM-IV. This is published by the American Psychiatric Association and it tends to be the most widely used.

- *The International Statistical Classification of Diseases and Related Health Problems,* 10th edition, referred to as ICD-10. This is the World Health Organisation system and it is the criteria that UK practitioners have tended to use most.

Although the criteria are similar, there are differences, especially in descriptions and in the number of symptoms. DSM-IV refers to ADHD, whereas the ICD-10 refers to hyperkinetic disorder.

The signs and symptoms may show themselves before your child is seven years of age, in some cases even sooner. If they display six or more symptoms from either of the basic categories – overactive and/or impulsive and inattentive – and these continue for at least six months, they may be said to have ADHD. These symptoms need to be identified at home, at school and in social settings to ensure they are consistent in your child's life, not just occurring in one type of environment.

Overactive and/or impulsive (hyperactive)

- Fidget or 'squirm' around in their seats a lot.

- Tend to leave their seats when they shouldn't do.

- Often climb or run when it isn't appropriate to do so.

- Find it hard to play quietly.

- Active all the time.

- Talk to excess.

- Blurt out answers to questions before the speaker has finished.

- Can't wait to take their turn.

- Interrupt others who are speaking or playing.

Inattentive (ADD type)

- Don't pay close attention to detail, or make careless mistakes in their schoolwork or other activities.

- Attention tends to wander during play or activities.

- Look as though they're not listening when spoken to.

- Fail to complete projects and to follow through on instructions in schoolwork or chores.

- Find it hard to organise activities and tasks.

- Avoid tasks like schoolwork or homework that involve mental effort.

- Tend to lose relevant materials for activities, like books, pencils or tools.

- Often distracted by what is going on around them.

- Forgetful.

'Often, boys can be more disruptive than girls in class, showing signs of boredom.'

Both types combined

The third category refers to the majority of ADHD children who are likely to have a mixture of hyperactivity, impulsiveness and inattentiveness.

Don't forget that many young children show signs of inattentiveness and may run around instead of sitting still and paying attention – this is quite normal behaviour. Often, boys can be more disruptive than girls in class, showing signs of boredom, while girls can spend time gazing out of the window and daydreaming. This doesn't mean they have ADHD.

What other characteristics might they have?

Children with ADHD can often be accident-prone because they have little sense of danger, are impulsive or impetuous and take risks from which the average child would steer clear. They don't always think before acting. They are likely to be the class underachievers because of their inability to concentrate, not necessarily because they aren't clever. They may not mix well with other children and can be undisciplined and antisocial, getting into all kinds of trouble that can follow them into their adult lives like petty crime, fighting and alcohol or substance abuse. They may attack other children, as well as self-harm. They may have difficulty sleeping, wet the bed, suffer eating disorders or experience anxiety and nervousness. This can be a depressing condition for some children.

Clumsy children and laterality

Some children may be clumsy, with poor co-ordination for fine motor tasks like tying shoelaces and writing legibly, and for gross motor tasks like hopping, skipping, kicking and catching balls. These children are usually cross-laterals whose laterality hasn't formed (although this normally resolves when the relevant part of the brain matures). It means that your child may be mixed-sided, for example left-handed but right-footed and right-eyed. Crossed hand/eye dominance may affect their performance in some sports where the field of vision might be restricted at times. They can also be mixed-handed, using either hand for different tasks, and can possess a lack of fixed dominance.

Language disorders

Sometimes speech disorders occur, including stuttering and issues with reading and writing. Philippa Greathead, a speech language pathologist from the Speech Language Learning Centre in Australia, gives a comprehensive overview of the types of language difficulties and learning styles for ADHD children, together with advice, in her article 'Language Disorders and Attention Deficit Hyperactivity Disorder'. You can read this on the ADDISS website, www.addiss.co.uk/languagedisorders.htm.

Philippa categorises the types of language difficulties shown by ADHD children as:

* Syntax (grammar).

* Semantics (meaning and organisation of words).

* Pragmatics (social use of language).

* Metalinguistics (reflecting objectively on language).

Related difficulties can include:

* Auditory processing (extracting information or following directions can be problematic).

* Metacognition (thinking about thinking and problem solving).

She points out that a child with ADHD may not respond to learning styles employed in schools, like sitting still and listening or having good reading and oral skills. They probably respond better in a one-to-one situation.

Lack of concentration

Research carried out at the University of Nottingham suggests that children with ADHD cannot turn off areas of their brain without first taking their medication or receiving high incentives. Children who do not have ADHD can close down the default mode network (DMN) in their brains when they are daydreaming and need to turn to something more productive. The findings showed why children with ADHD sometimes can't concentrate and how incentives and medication worked in a similar way to produce better concentration.

Researcher Dr Elizabeth Liddle said, 'The common complaint about children with ADHD is that "he can concentrate and control himself fine when he wants to", so some people just think the child is being naughty when he misbehaves. We have shown that this may be a very real difficulty for them. The off-switch for their "internal world" seems to need a greater incentive to function properly and allow them to attend to their task.'

How do others react?

Dr Nikos Myttas, consultant child and adolescent psychiatrist at Finchley Memorial Hospital, London, lists the sorts of reactions that ADHD children are likely to receive on account of their behaviour:

- Lazy.

- Underachievers.

- Not reaching their potential.

- Unpredictable.

- Disorganised.

- Erratic.

- Loud.

- Unfocused.

- Scatterbrained.

- Undisciplined.

- Uncontained.

You may even be blamed for poor parenting skills. This doesn't explain how your other children, if any, have grown up to be perfectly well behaved and easy to get along with. It is hard to defend such allegations, especially if they're made by an authority figure or health professional, as many parents may wind up feeling too guilty to challenge them.

Action points

■ Keep an eye on your child if you suspect they are behaving differently to children of their age group and development.

■ Use the checklist and note symptoms and their regularity.

■ Begin to keep a diary so that you have an accurate record of incidents, meetings with professionals and action taken. It will give you a good picture of the train of events and outcomes, which you may later need to refer to.

■ If contacting teachers, it's a good idea to put your intentions in writing so that you have copies of letters detailing all your actions.

■ If your child's behaviour is impairing the quality of their life and of those around them, and disrupting the atmosphere in your home, it may be time to ask for a diagnosis.

Summing Up

Being aware of the core symptoms outlined in the diagnostic criteria used by health professionals will help you to identify whether your child may need an assessment for ADHD. Keeping your own checklist will be helpful, as will noting down incidents and other observations in your diary. Remember though that many young children can be excessively energetic and may well display some of these symptoms anyway. They will grow out of them as they mature. However, if your child continues to persist in such behaviour to the extent that it makes their lives more difficult at home, socially and at school, then it's time to seek help.

Chapter Three
What Do We Do Next?

Diagnosing ADHD children

This can be a long and drawn-out process involving a battery of tests, observations and consultations with specialists. ADHD can reveal itself in mild, moderate and severe forms and, unfortunately, there isn't one particular biological or psychological test that can give you a diagnosis. ADHD is a complex clinical condition and the result of an assessment will be a clinical diagnosis. However, a variety of other conditions need to be ruled out first.

First steps

There are two routes to follow that will eventually lead you to a diagnosis.

- Contact your GP and tell them about your concerns. They can't diagnose ADHD themselves but they can make referrals to the appropriate specialists. You may find your GP will suggest other reasons for your child's behaviour, like problems at home, mixing with the wrong people, the 'terrible twos or threes' or not enough exercise. You are entitled to a second opinion, so don't be afraid to ask for one if you're not satisfied. You don't have to spend money on a private consultation either – a second opinion will be available under the National Health Service (NHS). This is your right.

- Contact your child's school. The school has to recognise the problem. They may already have done so and can themselves make the referral for a statutory assessment.

'You are entitled to a second opinion, so don't be afraid to ask for one if you're not satisfied.'

Seeing the consultants

The NHS Trust in your area will have a Child and Adolescent Mental Health Service (CAMHS) that includes psychiatrists, therapists and psychologists for under 18-year-olds. These are the only people who can diagnose ADHD and prescribe medicines for it, so it's important to push for a referral to CAMHS for a psychiatric assessment.

However, it's not uncommon in some areas to find huge waiting lists because there may be only one or two psychiatrists or psychologists covering thousands of people in the area. It isn't unknown for parents to have to wait as long as three years for an appointment. In some areas though, community paediatricians may specialise in ADHD.

CAMHS will carry out assessments and intelligence tests and attempt to rule out alternative reasons for your child's behaviour, which they will compare to your child's peer group. They will want to ascertain if your child is underperforming at school, even though their intellect may be normal and they may have no specific learning difficulties. Psychometric tests will help to expose any specific learning difficulties like dyslexia.

Your child will undergo a physical examination and tests for short-term memory, concentration and problem-solving skills. The team will go into the family background as well as your child's history at school. You may have to see them several times and they will also look at reports from other people, like your spouse or partner and all your child's teachers.

If your referral goes through your school, their special educational needs co-ordinator (SENCO) will help to co-ordinate this profiling from the school and may visit you in your home. After including their own narrative, they will submit the forms to CAMHS. If the answers to the questionnaires are all at the top of the spectrum, this is a strong signal that an assessment is necessary. If they come out at the lower end, then it probably isn't and you may have to repeat the exercise again six months later.

The diagnostic team

A team of health professionals may be involved in your child's diagnosis and treatment. Among them may be:

- GP.

- Child psychiatrist – deals with children's mental health.

- Paediatrician – a specialist in children's illnesses.

- Teacher.

- Neuropsychologist – assesses the links between the brain and behaviour. In addition to assessments, they provide information on how best to deal with changes in the brain due to accident or illness.

- Child psychologist – explores and understands the working of a child's mind and behaviour.

- Paediatric neurologist – specialises in how a child's brain works.

- Psychiatric social worker – trained to understand how the environment impacts on mental disorders.

- Educational psychologist – trained to combine psychology with educational issues. They can carry out IQ and other tests to define strengths and weaknesses, work with the school on the most appropriate strategies, contribute to statementing and offer counselling.

- Speech and language specialist – to ensure that your child is diagnosed correctly with ADHD and that they are not experiencing speech and language difficulties for other reasons.

- Audiologist – specialises in hearing loss and balance difficulties.

- Opthalmologist – specialises in diseases of the eye.

What are these tests?

- The diagnostic criteria mentioned in chapter 2 (DSM-IV or ICD-10) is used as part of this process. In the UK, ICD-10 is usually preferred and the sub-type hyperkinetic disorder used.

- Some examinations can show the difference between ADHD, mood disorders and learning difficulties.

- Questionnaires are designed to give a clear picture of your child's behaviour, emotions and relationships, which in ADHD children would be expected to be far more problematic than those displayed by children of their age and sex. Parents' and teachers' questionnaires include:
    - Achenbach Child Behaviour Checklists – these screen for a number of symptoms displayed by children like attention and aggression.
    - Barkley ADHD Rating Scale – a checklist showing symptom severity at home and school.
    - Conners Teacher and Parent Rating Scales.
    - DuPaul ADHD Rating Scale – a checklist showing symptom severity.
    - Edelbrock Child Attention Problems Rating Scale.
- Psychometric tests are timed tests that measure intellectual ability for thinking and reasoning.
- Tests showing persistence and attention, such as:
    - The Paired Association Learning Test.
    - Continuous Performance Test – for example, the Gordon Diagnostic System – to measure and compare impulse, vigilance and distraction issues.

'Other conditions can be common with ADHD and co-existing (often referred to as co-morbid) conditions can easily be overlooked.'

Can other conditions show up?

Other conditions can be common with ADHD and co-existing (often referred to as co-morbid) conditions can easily be overlooked, so they need to be checked out. Any of these that show up will need treating on their own account.

About half of ADHD children may have one or more of the following:

Affective disorder

ADHD children are unable to control their emotions and can explode with excessively angry outbursts. You may find these outbursts frightening and they can continue for a long time and become quite violent. Afterwards, your child may feel sorry and ashamed but they don't have the power to control these episodes at the time. Some may not remember what happened or develop an attitude.

Anxiety disorder

Panic attacks can occur in extreme situations but in general your child may worry and feel frightened. This can show with physical sensations like rapid heartbeats, the feeling of a lump in the throat, abdominal pains or diarrhoea. They are often perfectionists who worry constantly about different things and they seek reassurance, which doesn't help them. They can display phobias about anything from going to school to being away from home.

Asperger's syndrome

Named after the Austrian doctor Hans Asperger in the 1940s, his work was only advanced in the 1990s. It is sometimes viewed by psychiatrists as a mild form of autism but most people see it as a specific condition. Sufferers find it difficult to interact with peers and in social situations, have poor non-verbal communication, display ritualistic or repetitive behaviour and can be sensitive to sensory experiences. They are unable to understand things from someone else's viewpoint. Their vocabulary can be highly developed but they have difficulties with pragmatics (social communication) and semantics (word meanings). Because of these characteristics, you may find health professionals using different names. Speech therapists may call it semantic-pragmatic disorder; educational psychologists, non-verbal learning disorder; psychiatrists, high functioning autism or pervasive developmental disorder. If you hear these terms used, ask if they mean Asperger's syndrome.

Conduct disorder

About 7% of ADHD children may also display this kind of extreme confrontational behaviour. It can show at around seven to eight years of age and mainly occurs in boys. Many develop this in their teens after oppositional defiant disorder (see page 39), which is milder. Loners prefer to operate on their own but mostly they belong to gangs or groups of boys like themselves.

Their behaviour can lead to criminal activities, including thieving, breaking and entering property, sexual assaults, knife and gun crime or collections, physical attacks and cruelty to people (often siblings) and animals. They may truant, tell lies and run away from home. They think nothing of setting fire to buildings, which may include the family home.

Depression

Some ADHD children suffer from depression because of their condition. If your child is depressed, they may keep their distance from your family and friends. They may stay in their room or seem rooted to the TV. They may be weepy and mope about, looking dejected and feeling bad about themselves. Some of these children may eventually self-harm or attempt suicide.

Developmental language delay

A speech therapist will test your child if they have difficulty speaking clearly, understanding language or combining words. The therapist will observe them speaking and carry out tests to diagnose the cause, but it's advisable to have their hearing tested beforehand.

Obsessive-compulsive disorder (OCD)

An ADHD child is five times more likely to have OCD than the average child. They are unable to control thoughts that recur and occupy their minds constantly. You may notice your child carrying out the same tasks repeatedly, like washing hands or counting backwards. They cannot help themselves and are compelled to do this. It is very distressing if you try to stop them, as they feel that this behaviour relieves their distress.

Oppositional defiant disorder

This is the milder form of defiant behaviour and about 25% of children with ADHD display its characteristics, such as refusal to do chores, homework, carry out instructions or conform to rules and regulations. Punishment isn't a deterrent and you may find your child persistently arguing with you and other adults and having the sort of wild temper tantrums you might expect from a much younger child. If you send them to their room, they may well climb out of the window. You may also find them bothering their siblings or other children at school, taking their belongings or hitting them. They tend to be resentful, blame others for their own behaviour, flare up at the slightest provocation and swear a lot.

Specific learning difficulties (SpLDs)

Dyslexia comes from the Greek 'dys' (difficulty) and 'lexis' (words). It is thought to be caused by an unusual wiring of brain cells affecting some brain functions, and remedial treatment needs to be combined with medication. Children with dyslexia will have reading, spelling and writing abilities that don't measure up to their intellectual ability. They may also have problems with numbers.

If your local education authority (LEA) is taking too long over an appointment, you can pay to have a private assessment, although you shouldn't need to do this. Check out private companies carefully, as some may not be sufficiently qualified or effective – word of mouth recommendation is best.

Dyslexia is very common with ADHD children. If your child has ADD, any learning difficulties may be attributed just to dyslexia because ADD/ADHD is viewed as a behavioural issue.

Some great achievers are known to be dyslexic, for example Susan Hampshire, Su Pollard, Tom Cruise, Michael Heseltine (names cited on www.dys-add.com). Around 25% show left hand preference, more than 70% are cross-laterals and more boys are affected than girls. They can develop behavioural problems through frustration if their needs aren't provided for or recognised and if they are labelled as 'lazy' or 'stupid'. Some of their characteristics, together with reading, writing and spelling difficulties, include:

- Confusion over places, times, dates.
- Clumsiness.
- Lack of concentration.
- Left/right confusion.

- Mirror writing.

- Number/letter reversal.

- Poor handwriting.

- Poor short-term memory for signs and symbols, maths tables, instructions, names, names to faces.

- Fastening buttons, shoelaces, ties.

- Undetermined hand preference.

Substance abuse

If your child shows signs of defiant behaviour, they may begin drinking alcohol or experimenting with soft drugs. Although medication for ADHD won't affect your child adversely, the effect of these substances may interfere with the beneficial effect ADHD medication may be having on their condition.

Researchers at the University of California, Los Angeles (UCLA) claim that children with ADHD are two or three times more likely than other children to develop addiction and substance abuse in adolescence and adulthood and find it harder to give up. They found no differences between boys and girls, race or ethnicity or the types of substances, which included nicotine, alcohol, marijuana, cocaine and other drugs.

Tic disorder

Tics are common to about 10% of children with ADHD. Simple motor tics consist of short repetitive twitches that occur in different parts of the face, neck and shoulders. Complex motor tics are more pronounced like jumping or stamping. Simple vocal tics consist of repeated sounds like grunting, clearing the throat or sniffing. Complex vocal tics involve repetition of words or phrases, some of them vulgar. Tic disorder is genetic and some genes are shared with ADHD genes. Tics can be triggered by ADHD medication, so this should be monitored if it is suspected.

Tourette's syndrome (or disorder)

Named after Dr George de la Tourette, a French neurologist in 1825, this is a neurological disorder characterised by multiple motor tics and one or more vocal tics that have persisted for one year. Most sufferers display a mild form and many youngsters will grow out of it. A lot of mythology surrounds Tourette's, mainly because of distorted media representations.

Gathering a mass of information about your child, their symptoms and their background should enable health professionals to make an accurate diagnosis so that the appropriate treatment can be recommended to help your child realise their true potential and improve their quality of life.

Summing Up

An assessment carried out in the early stages of ADHD is obviously going to be beneficial to your child's wellbeing and ability to function in the world around them. It will be helpful for you to know that this distressing condition has a name and that any other co-existing conditions will also benefit from identification and treatment. It isn't always so cut and dried though, as co-operation and effectiveness of health trusts and education departments differ depending on where you live and the sort of resources that are available.

Chapter Four

What Causes ADHD?

Parliamentary questions

In November 2007, Baroness Susan Greenfield, Professor of Pharmacology at the University of Oxford, asked the House of Lords to look at how ADHD was being diagnosed and treated, considering the great increase in children being diagnosed with it over the last 20 years. She was told that it was unclear whether ADHD in children was on the increase or whether public awareness had made it more apparent. This, however, raised the possibility of a new review across government departments.

Baroness Greenfield wondered whether the changes to our ways of living could be contributing to the increase and if the time was ripe for an inquiry exploring the actual causes of ADHD. Diverse factors ranging from diet through to screen-based activity, and how they were changing the way both children and adults interact socially, needed considering. Baroness Greenfield commented that children lived faster-paced, more interactive existences nowadays and that they might be finding it harder 'to sit still' at school.

Although the figures may appear to be mounting, especially in the USA, critics have raised the possibility that in the past children have been incorrectly diagnosed or have not been diagnosed or noted at all.

The causes

Genetic research

What does cause ADHD? Nobody knows the answer to this question for

'Although the figures may appear to be mounting, especially in the USA, critics have raised the possibility that in the past, children have been incorrectly diagnosed or have not been diagnosed or noted at all.'

certain but the general consensus, particularly judging from twin and adoption research, is that it is genetic and that the gene can be inherited. Research has shown that about 25% of close relatives to someone with ADHD will also have the condition, compared to 5% in the community. Parents and siblings of ADHD children are four or five times more likely to have it.

Researchers from around the globe launched the ADHD Molecular Genetics Network in 1999 to pool their genetic knowledge and standardise assessment tests. Several defective genes associated with ADHD have been noted.

Attention has been centred on changes in genes concerned with dopamine pathways in the brain, such as the dopamine transporter gene (which stimulants like Ritalin – the drug most often used to treat ADHD – bind to) and the D4 receptor gene. Neurotransmitters – dopamine and noradrenaline (norepinephrine) – are chemicals that carry messages in the brain and it's thought that these don't work as efficiently as they do in children who don't have ADHD. However, scans have shown that Ritalin can correct these imbalances.

However, in 2010, breakthrough genetic research looking at gene variation at Cardiff University revealed that ADHD had genetic links. Researchers found that some sections of DNA in children with ADHD were duplicated, while others were missing. An overlap in segments implicated in autism and schizophrenia, suggested that ADHD could be a neurodevelopmental disorder.

Professor Anita Thapar, from the School of Medicine, said, 'Too often, people dismiss ADHD as being down to bad parenting or poor diet. As a clinician, it was clear to me that this was unlikely to be the case. Now we can say with confidence that ADHD is a genetic disease and that the brains of children with this condition develop differently to those of other children.'

The findings provoked a furore, its detractors insisting that environmental factors also played a part in the equation and there was no single gene as yet known for ADHD.

'Could the changes to our ways of living be contributing to this increase? The time is ripe for an inquiry exploring the actual causes of ADHD.'

Baroness Susan Greenfield, Lords Hansard, 14 November 2007.

Cognitive testing

Masses of research has been carried out over the last 30 years on cognitive abilities in ADHD children. Compared to their peers, these children show less activity in part of the brain's frontal lobes and have deficiencies in their executive functions. Executive functions are linked to the frontal cortex and affect planning, response control and decision-making. They affect your child's ability to behave in an appropriate manner, especially socially, and to think before acting.

The frontal lobes

The frontal lobes lie at the front of the brain and are connected to other parts of the brain by neural pathways, which in ADHD children don't function as well as they should do. A reduction in blood flow to areas like the caudate nucleus (involved in memory, learning and feedback functions) and the frontal lobes indicates abnormalities. The frontal lobes deal with a variety of important functions, including:

- Personality.
- Intelligence.
- Forward planning.
- Problem-solving.
- Impulsivity.
- Understanding other's behaviour.
- Decision-making.

It is beyond the scope of this book to go into great detail about the workings of the brain and how its functions are affected by the ADHD genes, but this brief mention of some dysfunctions that occur in ADHD children may clarify the results of scientific research to find answers to the often-asked question 'Why does my child have ADHD?'

Scientists worldwide are researching new ways of diagnosing and treating ADHD sufferers all the time. Many theories have been put forward for its cause – some have been disproved and others are leading to new areas for research. The prevalence and character of ADHD is thought to be the same universally, with the highest incidence in the Ukraine (around 20%).

The IMAGEN project

Early in 2007, the MRC Social Genetic and Developmental Psychiatry Research Centre based at the Institute of Psychiatry, King's College, London, launched the IMAGEN project at the Institute. This is a major international study for European clinical investigators and molecular geneticists. It aims to compile medical data and DNA from 14-year-olds, including those with ADHD and their families, in a bid to amass a resource for identifying the genes that cause the disorder. A battery of psychological tests are included to study the links between environmental factors and genetics. It is likely to take five years to gather this information from 2,000 youngsters, their parents and siblings, and to compare the similarities and differences between them. However, it will be a major research resource, enabling scientists to get closer to understanding the disorder.

What can brain scans tell us?

Three types of scan have been used in long-term studies of areas of the brain that might reveal a physical explanation for ADHD. The scans can't diagnose ADHD but they can help scientists to understand more about how the brain works in relevant areas.

Magnetic resonance imaging (MRI)

This scanner uses radio and magnetic waves so there is no danger from radiation. Strong radio waves go through your child's body as they lie in a large (and noisy) cylindrical magnet. Signals received from their body are converted into pictures that show up all the body's tissues, or areas surrounded by bone tissue like the brain, from any angle. This process has been in use since the 1980s.

Positron emission tomography (PET)

Nuclear medicine is used in this type of scan to identify physiological and chemical changes. The radioactive substances used last only a short while (twenty minutes to two hours). This process was developed in the 1970s and is thought to be invaluable in evaluating the brain.

Single-photo emission computed tomography (SPECT)

SPECT is also a nuclear medicine technique used in functional brain imaging. A radioactive tracer is injected so that gamma rays are emitted by the patient and picked up by a nuclear gamma camera, which produces 3D images of the brain.

What do the scientists say?

In 1990, an American study of the neurobiological effects of ADHD using brain imaging found that the brains of people with ADHD used glucose – its major source of energy – at a lower rate than normal. This was pronounced in the part of the brain responsible for inhibitory reactions, motor control, attention and writing. It was discovered that ADHD children had a three-year delay, on average, of brain maturity in the cortex compared to their peers, and although their brains eventually begin to develop at the same pace as non-ADHD children, the ADHD children never manage to catch up. The cortex, the outer layer of the brain, is responsible for planning and attention.

Other suggested causes

A variety of other causes for ADHD have been studied, ranging from environmental factors to faulty diet and food intolerances. It's a good idea to know about them so that you can get a fuller picture of all the possibilities.

Environmental factors

- Smoking and drinking – indulging in alcohol and tobacco during pregnancy have been suggested as possible factors that can affect the foetus and the future health of the unborn child.

- High lead levels – although lead is no longer used in making toy soldiers or in paint, it is thought that young children may still face some risk from toxins in old buildings containing lead plumbing or lead paint that still exists under the paintwork.

Birth complications

- Premature babies who are born with low birth weight could be at risk.

'The belief that ADHD is caused by bad parenting or outside factors alone can no longer be accepted.'

- The incidence of ADHD children has been found to be higher among younger mothers.

- Babies whose mothers are stressed during pregnancy have a greater chance of developing ADHD and behavioural problems. They also find it hard to form relationships when they start school, according to research carried out by the Institute of Psychiatry, King's College, London.

Accidents affecting the brain

- Children who have been in accidents and suffered brain injuries as a result are said to show similar symptoms to those with ADHD, but few children diagnosed with ADHD appear to have suffered such accidents.

- Brain damage caused in utero or in your child's early years could be responsible for ADHD later.

Hearing impairments

- Children who have hearing problems could be at risk from developing ADHD.

Food allergies and intolerances

- Research clashes in this area and camps are divided. Sugar and food additives play a big part in the argument, as does a lack of fish oils in the diet. Some studies show that cutting sugar and additives out of your child's diet can help alleviate some of the symptoms, whereas others find they have no effect one way or the other. Diet and nutrition are very much in the public eye at the moment, so much so that the subject merits a chapter to itself where we can look at it in closer detail (see chapter 7). While these substances may not be the cause of ADHD, they may well play some part in your child's behaviour and mental state.

Gender

- Boys are more likely to be diagnosed with ADHD than girls. It's often thought that the sort of rowdy behaviour displayed by boys tends to be noted more and that girls tend to display symptoms of ADD rather than ADHD, being quieter and inattentive rather than boisterous or disruptive.

Too much TV?

- A number of researchers have studied the effects of overexposure to TV in young children to see if this can contribute to ADHD. The evidence for this is slim but it has been suggested that if you let your one to three-year-old watch TV for several hours each day, it could create attention issues and ADHD in the future.

Sleep loss

Sleep loss among pre-school age children can produce ADHD symptoms in kindergarten. These children can be more hyperactive and less attentive than the other children, according to private American research. ADHD sufferers often have trouble getting to sleep and staying asleep, or experience night fears, nightmares and sleepwalking.

'Some studies show that cutting sugar and additives out of your child's diet can help alleviate some of the symptoms.'

Action points

■ 'After diagnosis, you have to become an expert – become the solution, not the problem'. Andrea Bilbow, ADDISS.

■ Attend conferences.

■ Learn as much as you can about the condition.

■ Find out about Disability Allowance and use the money to educate yourself.

■ Join a support group like ADDISS.

Summing Up

The belief that ADHD is caused by bad parenting or outside factors alone can no longer be accepted. We now know from the vast amount of research investigations into the brain's functions and development, using the most advanced technology available, that children with ADHD have impairments in their brain functioning in certain areas that are different from other children of the same age. It's encouraging that research is ongoing worldwide, that scientists may not be far off finding some solutions which could lead to better diagnosis and treatment of ADHD, and that some day even a cure may be found.

Chapter Five

The Ritalin Controversy

If your child has been diagnosed with ADHD, a variety of treatments will be suggested. Each case is individual, based upon the symptoms and needs of the child. Co-morbid conditions will need to be treated separately.

A combination of drugs and talking therapies is generally recommended, but that doesn't mean you can't search around for alternative treatments to complement them. You may be told that homeopathy, for example, doesn't work because there is no substance in the medicine. But you may feel that anything is worth trying if it will help to relax your child and make them feel better, especially if they have no harmful side effects. If alternative therapies improve their wellbeing, you may feel that the way in which they work is immaterial.

Types of treatment

A combination of medical and behavioural treatments work alongside educational support at school and parental support at home. Medication can help to balance the brain's chemicals, but both drugs and the suggestion that diet can help alleviate symptoms are sources of controversy among the medical profession, parents and the media. Other forms of therapy, complementary therapies and nutrition are treated separately in chapters 6 and 7.

What kind of medication is involved?

Drugs aren't compulsory or always necessary, but sometimes they are used and parents report a vast improvement in their children's behaviour. They can't cure your child but they can alleviate the symptoms. New guidelines recommend drug treatment for children and young people with moderate to

'I think in 10 years' time we will say that ADHD was too simple an explanation for many children . . . We will ask ourselves what we were thinking giving these children amphetamines.'

Dr Gwynedd Lloyd, head of Educational Studies, University of Edinburgh, BBC Radio Scotland, *News 24*, 3 September 2006.

severe ADHD levels to be given by specialists only in extreme cases. Please see your GP for information and advice on the types of medication available; the following is only for general information.

Medication

Psychostimulants (central nervous system stimulants (CNS)) tend to be used in the main because they balance the brain's chemicals in the area for control and inhibitions. They lift mood and stimulate neurotransmitter production. Neurotransmitters are chemicals in the brain that send messages from one nerve cell to another.

- Methylphenidate is the stimulant most in use in the UK. Ritalin is the one we hear about often but it is not much in use here. The slow release version, Ritalin SR, is not licensed but can be obtained off licence. Dexamphetamine is also a stimulant, similar to methylphenidate. Attention should be improved and hyperactivity reduced but both can have side effects. Ritalin is no longer the most widely used methylphenidate.

- Concerta XL is another psychostimulant (and a brand of methylphenidate). These are extended release, so just one tablet in the morning is necessary. Attention and behaviour are improved, however this comes with a host of warnings about side effects and existing conditions that may worsen. NICE recommends that children under six should not take these drugs.

- Equasym and Medikinet are also psychostimulants (and a brand of methylpenidate). Their side effects are the same as Ritalin's.

- Dexamfetamine. Dexedrine influences the neurotransmitter noradrenaline (norepinephrine) and inhibits dopamine reuptake. It can be used by adolescents and children over three years of age.

- Atomoxetine. Strattera is not a psychostimulant but it works in a similar way. It boosts noradrenaline in the brain, which in turn helps concentration and controls impulsive behaviour. It is used by adolescents and children over six years of age.

'Three weeks later, I discovered I could think before I spoke; that there was a box to put the thoughts into, and then speak them. After a year I stopped taking it [Ritalin], and I could still use the box . . . At 18 I remember saying for the first time, "I like myself".'

Daniel Bedingfield, prescribed Ritalin, aged 18. *The Guardian*, 28 July 2003.

Tricyclic antidepressants (TCAs) are used to relieve depression, a symptom of ADHD. They inhibit the overstimulation of the nerve cells by neurotransmitters such as noradrenaline and serotonin in the brain. 'Tricyclic' refers to three rings in the drug's chemical structure.

* Imipramine* – Tofranil relieves depression and anxiety. It inhibits noradrenaline reuptake.

Clonidine* is used for hypertension and is recommended to be taken towards the end of the day. It helps with sleeping difficulties, which can be caused by stimulants, decreases hyperactivity, impulsivity and aggressive behaviour. It is usually taken with Ritalin or Dexedrine.

*These drugs are unlicensed for ADHD treatment and would only be suggested after referral to tertiary services when patients fail to respond to methylphenidates.

How to manage the dosage

Some people feel that giving drugs to young children in large doses over a long period, especially amphetamines, is wrong. For example, some children have been taking Ritalin for over 10 years to help them calm down and concentrate on their education. This seems to work in the short term but your child may need many pills every day before they take effect. You will need to talk to your doctor for more information.

* Immediate release tablets are taken two or three times a day in small doses (Ritalin/Equasym). Fast release drugs last up to about four hours.

* Modified release tablets are taken once in the morning (Concerta XL). The drugs are released gradually during the day. Slow-release drugs last for about 12 hours.

* Getting the dose right is important. If your child takes too much they could become like zombies and lose their appetites. After a while, the medication wears off and the body gets used to it.

* In America, methylphenidate patches (Daytrana), introduced for six to 12-year-olds in long-acting form, last about nine hours.

Initially, your child may be given small doses that may be gradually increased, and they will need to be monitored by specialists on a regular basis. Sometimes a 'medicine holiday' can be suggested for a short period if the treatment is seen to be working well so that your child's reactions without the drug can be noted. However, if the drugs are stopped, your child should always come off them gradually.

NICE guidelines

The National Institute for Clinical Excellence (NICE) produces guidelines on preventing and treating illnesses and the promotion of good health. Their guidelines are put together by experts that include carers and service users, but they are essentially guidelines and not instructions. They cover many specific illnesses, but it is the clinical guidelines on ADHD that you need to know about. You can obtain and consult their summaries by contacting them (see information below).

NICE produced guidance on the use of methylphenidate in October 2000, which maintained that ADHD children who didn't take it could benefit from doing so. A review was produced in March 2006 on drugs in the treatment of ADHD in England and Wales, entitled 'Methylphenidate, atomoxetine and dexamfetamine for attention deficit hyperactivity disorder (ADHD) in children and adolescents'. These documents can be obtained from NICE at 71 High Holborn, London WC1V 6NA or viewed and downloaded from their website at www.nice.org.uk/TA098 0845 003 7780 or by phoning the NHS Response Line on 0870 1555 455 quoting N1011.

New guidelines on the diagnosis and management of ADHD in children aged three and over, young people and adults were published in September 2008 (clinical guideline 72). The recommendations include:

▓ Changes to diet.

▓ Behavioural interventions at school.

▓ Parents and carers to attend group or individual-based parent-training/education programmes and group cognitive behavioural therapy and social skills training, rather than drug-based interventions. NICE stress that this is not an indicator of poor parenting skills but is an important part of managing children who may be harder to parent on account of their ADHD symptoms.

The 2008 guidelines can be obtained from NICE publications on 0845 003 7783 or by email from publications@nice.org.uk, quoting N1684 for a quick reference guide and N1685 for 'Understanding NICE Guidance'. They can be viewed and downloaded from the NICE website at www.nice.org.uk/CG072. They were reviewed in November, 2011. The review recommendation was that the guideline should not be updated at this time. The guideline will be reviewed again in July 2014.

NICE criteria

NICE guidelines include details of the medications and outline when a child or adolescent might take specific ones depending on certain criteria, such as:

* Other conditions from which your child may suffer.

* The sort of side effects that might affect them.

* Whether taking them during school hours would create any problems.

* The danger of others taking them.

* Your child's preference, or your own.

* The importance of reminders to take them regularly and to adopt positive attitudes towards them.

These guidelines were due for review October 2011. Please check with NICE.

Prescriptions and costs

According to NICE, 220,000 prescriptions for stimulants like methylphenidate and dexamfetamine were issued in 1998, costing £5 million net. By 2004, this had risen to 418,300 prescriptions, costing the nation £13 million. This was put down to the rise in diagnoses. In the 2006 guidelines, it was suggested that about 366,000 children and adolescents in England and Wales met the diagnostic criteria for ADHD, although not all of them would need medication.

In the 12 months to June 2009, the cost of prescribing methylphenidate had risen to £21,638,372, an increase of 6%. However, since April 2007, hospitals have reduced their usage.

Scotland

According to NHS Quality Improvement Scotland (NHS QIS), prescriptions for Ritalin rose from 69 to 603 per 10,000 between 1996 and 2004. It was thought that recognition of ADHD may have accounted for this but QIS were by no means sure whether it was because of under or over-prescribing and significant regional variations couldn't be accounted for. Figures increased by 20.1% from 49,258 to 59,461 between 2005/6 and 2006/7.

The QIS report 'ADHD – Services Over Scotland', produced in March 2007, details a government project to identify services for ADHD in Scottish regions, with the aim of improving the quality and care delivered by NHS Scotland. A copy can be obtained direct from NHS QIS (see the help list) or downloaded from their website on www.nhshealthquality.org.

Clinical guidelines for NHS Scotland are developed by the Scottish Intercollegiate Guidelines Network (SIGN). Their guidelines, 'Attention Deficit and Hyperkinetic Disorders in Children and Young People' (2001/updated 2005), includes diagnoses, assessments and management. It covers treatment, mainly for co-morbid conditions, drugs and their possible side effects. The report can be seen on their website www.sign.ac.uk and you can download copies.

Northern Ireland

Similar guidelines to NICE are available from the Department of Health in Belfast or from their website at www.dhsspsni.gov.uk.

Concerns have been voiced about the rise in Ritalin and Concerta prescriptions in Northern Ireland, where access to psychotherapy and other 'talking therapies' isn't easily available. Families travel from afar to receive these therapies in Belfast at the Northern Ireland ADHD Support Centre, which claims that 600 children attend their programmes.

'By inhibiting impulsive behaviour in children with ADHD it [Ritalin] allows them to socialise and develop normally . . . Despite the risks, the medication can work for some children.'

Dr Dave Coghill, senior lecturer in Child and Adolescent Psychiatry, University of Dundee, BBC Radio Scotland, *News 24*, 3 September 2006

Is there cause for concern?

In Canada, Adderall XR was suspended in 2005 because of concerns about unexplained deaths among children taking it. However, it made a comeback six months later but was no longer prescribed to children with heart abnormalities. The same condition applies now in America.

Questions have also been raised about possible addiction to psychostimulants and the possibility that other children might attempt to take medication used by ADHD children at school or in the home.

A United Nations report expressed concerns in 1995 about dramatic and continued increases in the use of Ritalin in the United States, where it amounts to about 90% of world consumption and production. There is also evidence of abuse and a black market that is feared may spread to other countries. The Federal Drugs Agency (FDA) in the USA has warned against its use and the US Drug Enforcement Administration (DEA) enforces licences for manufacture, distribution and prescribing it, prohibiting prescription refills. Each state is free to add extra limits to their control.

In November 2007, a BBC Panorama programme revealed that around 500,000 ADHD children received no treatment. Those that do – about 55,000 – had been prescribed Ritalin and Concerta, many for long-term use, at a cost to the NHS of £28 million. It was also revealed that American research at the University of Buffalo showed only short-term use could be beneficial. The study, carried out by 18 top authorities in ADHD at six university medical centres and hospitals, followed the treatment of 600 children from the 1990s. They found that three years of treatment was sufficient and that those continuing long-term had stunted growth and had ceased to benefit from the medication.

Critics of the programme, mainly ADHD sufferers who felt they had benefitted from medication, emphasised that Ritalin was not known to be addictive, there were rarely any withdrawal symptoms when the drug was stopped and ADHD medication was well supervised and controlled by medical experts, and not doled out like sweets as had been suggested. The programme was withdrawn from circulation after complaints about its inaccuracies. An earlier Panorama programme in 2000, *Kids on Pills,* looked at the rise in children diagnosed with

' . . . There is a lack of data on the impact that treatment has had on ADHD. It is perhaps not a recent phenomenon, but Ritalin, for example, has only been prescribed since 1988. Sadly, the long-term data is currently lacking.'

Baroness Royall of Blaisdon, Lords *Hansard,* 14 November 2007.

ADHD and its treatment with Ritalin. Prescriptions had risen from less than 16,000 in 1995 to nearly 140,000 in 1998, with 3 million children taking it in the USA.

A discussion about ADHD in the House of Lords, sparked off by Baroness Susan Greenfield's concerns about 'long-term inefficacy of Ritalin' raised by the American research, revealed that a European review of its safety and effectiveness had been underway since June 2007. It was pointed out that Ritalin hadn't been in use long enough to produce any significant data. However, one concern was that Ritalin was being used and abused by non-ADHD students due to its stimulant properties.

NICE recommend that medication should only be used in extreme cases of ADHD. For some parents, Ritalin has been labelled a 'chemical cosh' because they fear that rather than modifying behaviour, it merely suppresses it.

Knowing about possible side effects

All the previously mentioned drugs have side effects, some more severe than others. They can only be obtained on prescription and your child's specialist will decide which ones are most suitable for them, if they feel that medication is necessary. It may not be.

The table opposite is given purely as information so that you are aware of the sort of side effects that could occur. Please see your doctor for professional medical advice and information. People react differently to medication so side effects may be either non-existent, short-lived or a problem, necessitating experiments with dosages or change of type.

NICE recommend regular monitoring for side effects.

Side effects	Medication	Higher Doses	Comments
Appetite loss	Ritalin Equasym Medikinet Dexedrine Concerta Strattera		Short period Same as Ritalin Adults and children
Constipation	Tofranil	Ritalin Equasym Medikinet	
Cough	Concerta		
Depression		Ritalin Equasym Medikinet	
Dizziness	Concerta Clonidine Strattera	Ritalin Equasym Medikinet	 Adults and children
Dry mouth	Tofranil Clonidine Strattera	Ritalin Equasym Medikinet	 Adults
Fatigue	Strattera		
Headaches	Concerta	Ritalin Equasym Medikinet	

'Drugs can't cure your child but they can alleviate the symptoms.'

Insomnia	Ritalin Dexedrine Equasym Medikinet Concerta		Short period
	Strattera		Adults
Irritability		Ritalin Equasym Medikinet	
Nausea	Clonidine Strattera	Ritalin Equasym Medikinet	Adults and children
Rash	Clonidine		
Sedation	Clonidine		
Sexual problems	Strattera		Adults Libido
Sinusitis	Concerta		
Sore throat	Concerta		
Stomach aches	Concerta	Ritalin Equasym Medikinet	
Stomach upsets	Strattera		Adults and children
Tics		Ritalin Equasym Medikinet	

Upper respiratory tract infection	Concerta		
Urinary problems	Strattera		Adults
Vomiting	Concerta Strattera		Adults and children

Many parents don't like the idea of their children taking psychostimulants, which are class B substances. Long-term effects can be a worry, as can tolerance levels, which require higher doses and can lead to withdrawal issues. However, in severe cases of ADHD they are reported to have a beneficial effect in calming down hyperactive children.

Other fears

Apart from possible side effects, there are other fears attached to drugs, such as misuse by siblings and peers, over-diagnosis or that they are being administered unnecessarily to give teachers and parents an easier life. Your child may even be bullied at school so that other pupils can take their medication and sell it, or they may sell it themselves. Ritalin can be sold for 50p to £3 and is on the police's top 10 list for thefts.

In the USA, Dr Jennifer Setlik, emergency doctor at Cincinnati Children's Hospital Medical Centre, Ohio and the author of a study published in Pediatrics, September 2009 said that parents 'should be aware of the potential for abuse of these medications for teens that have and haven't been prescribed them,' and she recommended parents should monitor the amount their children use. ADHD drug abuse had risen 76% from 1998 to 2005 and prescription rates rose around 80% for children and teenagers and 86% for 10 to 19-year-olds. Prescription medications are used most by teens to get high, after marijuana.

It's important for parents and teachers to understand which drugs are likely to be used and what side effects they need to look out for. Teachers also need to support children with ADHD if doses need to be taken during the school day, although taking the slow-release version means children don't need to take medication to school.

Summing Up

Masses of research is ongoing worldwide, much of it in universities whose funding comes from the drug companies. As a parent, you have choices and, armed with the appropriate knowledge, those choices will be informed ones. However, it isn't all doom and gloom, for questions are being asked by senior members of government in the UK and Europe that may result eventually in improved diagnosis and treatment for your child.

Remember, always seek professional medical advice from your doctor.

Chapter Six

Talking Therapies and Alternatives

Treatment packages

A package of treatments is usually suggested to alleviate symptoms, to help your child enjoy a more fulfilling life and to reduce stress at home. They may be prescribed medication if their condition is serious enough, which should give parents, teachers and health specialists time to assess how best to manage their case. Some children will need behavioural and psychological therapy, with or without the medication, and backup support from home and school. Don't forget that other members of the family can be involved in therapy.

Therapies that may be suggested to you include:

- Psychiatry.
- Psychology.
- Behavioural therapy geared to changing your child's behaviour and creating management strategies for your family.
- Social skills training to help your child socialise better and to communicate with other children.

What do they all do?

The different 'talking therapies' can be confusing, so it's worth taking a look at some of them.

'There are only two ways to live your life. One is as though nothing is a miracle. The other is as though everything is a miracle.'
Albert Einstein.

Psychiatry

Psychiatrists qualify as medical doctors before specialising in mental health conditions, and can prescribe medication and recommend other treatments. Your GP or social services can refer you to a psychiatrist (see chapter 3).

After carrying out the assessment, the child psychiatrist will be in charge of your child's diagnosis and treatment package and they will decide which, if any, medication to prescribe. They will also liaise with the clinical psychologist.

Psychology

'Many parents complain about the length of time they have to wait under the NHS for talking therapies.'

A psychologist will deal with your child's behavioural issues. Psychologists study motivation, thoughts, feelings and behaviour. They need to have an accredited psychology degree, followed by post-graduate training relevant to the specific area in which they choose to practice, such as a doctorate in clinical or educational psychology if they work with children.

- Educational psychologists will deal with your child's educational difficulties at school, such as reading, writing, spelling, language disorders and any specific learning difficulties (see chapter 8).

- Clinical psychologists will use counselling and other therapies to help your child to change their way of thinking so they will think and behave more positively.

Psychotherapy

Psychotherapists usually have a post-graduate qualification in psychotherapy and they often come from other health disciplines. They will talk to your child and help them to explore their thoughts, feelings and behaviour and any emotional or psychological issues that concern them. Your child may not be consciously aware of some of these feelings and thoughts and may need to look at their past experiences and learn to develop some coping strategies to deal with them.

Psychotherapists can help with:

- Anxiety.

- Depression.

- Inability to form relationships with others.

- Low self-esteem.

- Mood swings.

- Panic attacks.

- Physical symptoms.

- Poor concentration.

- Underachievement at school.

Counselling

Counsellors are usually qualified to diploma level and can help your child to look at their problems from alternative angles. They examine your child's behaviour and actions, and consider various other options. By exploring their issues in this way, your child may be able to find more positive and satisfactory ways of managing their behaviour. Effectively, your child will be encouraged to work out their own pathway for themselves.

You may also feel the need for a series of counselling sessions to help you to cope with some of the issues involved in dealing with your child's ADHD. If you have other children, they may also benefit from counselling if their sibling's ADHD or the atmosphere at home is affecting them.

Behavioural therapy

Behavioural therapy can show you how to employ management strategies that will help you to deal with your child's behaviour. To reinforce the need for them to behave well, token rewards and timeouts may be given to your child for good and bad behaviour respectively. This therapy can include all carers involved in your child's support, such as teachers and family members, as well as the child. Teachers can learn how to plan activities and to praise your child when they do well.

Cognitive behavioural therapy (CBT)

The word 'cognitive' means the way in which you think about yourself and the things that happen to you. Behaviour means how you act and react to situations.

CBT involves stepping back and regarding thoughts, feelings and physical sensations before acting. If your child is not on medication, they may be too hyperactive to be able to do this.

This therapy is about changing your child's thinking, but it can be a long process before stepping back becomes a new way of behaving for them.

Social skills training

Social skills training will guide your child through strategies needed to mix well with others in social situations. They will learn about the effects their behaviour may have on other people and the need to change this for more positive behaviour that is socially acceptable. Role play is usually involved in this.

Parents and family support

Other support involving parents and the family are dealt with in chapter 9, while diet and nutrition are covered in chapter 7.

Other therapies under research

Other therapies are being piloted and are in the early stages of research. Current results have been encouraging for ADHD.

They include:

- Neuropathy – EEG biofeedback has been used in the USA for ADHD. Research has found it to work quite well for ADHD but further studies are needed. It is thought to help disturbed sleep, anxiety, depression, attention and uncontrolled emotion by training the brain to regulate its own activity.

- Dance therapy – Therapeutic eurythmy, a holistic movement therapy, is thought to aid concentration, attention span, co-ordination, social behaviour and working speed for ADHD children.

- Speech and language therapy – because of the lack of services in this area, the University of Sheffield has looked at types of delivery to show how beneficial they would be to ADHD children and adolescents.

ADHD coaching

Coaching for ADHD is more behaviour modification than a therapy. It is becoming very popular for helping ADHD patients and involves working with the coach to learn new types of behaviour so that the sort of ADHD behaviours producing underachievement and low self-esteem can be turned around. The idea is that with the coach's support and encouragement, your child's attitude should change to a more positive approach that will raise their self-confidence and ability to realise their potential. It is said to give ADHD children a new-found sense of achievement.

Many children have blocks about attempting tasks that seem too daunting for them. The coach would work towards eliminating your child's negative language and views about themselves, replacing them with positive attitudes. Combined with other treatments, it is said to be very effective. Tasks with goals are set between visits for your child to achieve in line with a contract and an action plan, which is set when the treatment begins.

It's important to find a coach who is knowledgeable and experienced in working with ADHD children and some of the co-morbid symptoms like dyslexia, dyspraxia and Asperger's syndrome.

Private help

Many parents complain about the length of time they have to wait under the NHS for talking therapies. After waiting months or years for an assessment, you may find it hard continuing to wait while your situation at home has become unbearable. This can seem like a setback and the pressure this puts you under can contribute to family arguments and even break-ups. Consequently, some parents seek private help because the NHS doesn't have enough therapists to deal with the amount of patients on their waiting lists.

If you go down the private route, try to find a therapist who has been personally recommended to you by someone you know and is experienced in dealing with ADHD patients, particularly children. Your doctor may be able to suggest someone or you could try one of the professional associations listed in the help list. Make sure they are fully trained and qualified in their specialism, that they belong to a recognised professional association and carry professional indemnity and public liability insurance.

Costs

It can be expensive to see a private therapist, particularly if regular visits are required for a long time. Try to find out initially how long your child will be expected to go for treatment and whether you have to pay them if you miss a session. Fees can vary enormously from about £30-£40 an hour upwards.

Alternative therapies

You may like to investigate some alternative therapies to complement your child's treatment. The advice for consulting private therapists is as above.

Some treatments have been found to be beneficial, especially for relaxation, but effectiveness can vary depending on the individual. What works for one person may not work for another and this is the same with traditional medicine.

Alternative therapy can complement the treatment advised by your specialists but it's important to let your alternative therapists know what treatment your child is having to ensure that it doesn't clash with any remedies they may use. There are some whacky therapies out there, along with therapies reported to be helpful and effective.

Research

Less research has been carried out on alternative therapies because of lack of funding, whereas pharmaceutical companies pour millions into traditional medical research. Some of those research results may be variable, some remain unpublished, some texts are taken out of context and sensationalised by the media and accusations of bias are often heard.

- Herbalism – herbs should only be administered by a qualified herbalist as they can be dangerous without the knowledge of their effects and how they may react with any prescribed medication. Some are good for insomnia or as a sedative, like valerian used in the short term. You can buy herbal teas like chamomile, valerian, hops, passion flower, green tea or lemon balm in any health food shop or supermarket.

- Homeopathy – this works on similar principles to vaccination but is given in pill form. It treats like with like to boost the body's own defences to deal with minute doses of the symptoms. Diagnosis is holistic and remedies are tailored for the child as an individual, not based on their ADHD symptoms alone. The substances are derived from plants and minerals, and are reported to have no side effects or to interfere with medications. Practitioners can be medical doctors who have had two further years of training or other qualified homeopaths.

- Hypnotherapy – this is said to be useful for controlling some symptoms like sleep problems, panic attacks or tics. It's got nothing to do with stage hypnotism but uses suggestion to condition the patient's subconscious mind to adopt more productive ways of dealing with issues.

- Meditation – there are numerous types and it can be done in groups or individually. Transcendental meditation involves repeating a mantra to quieten the mind, producing a feeling of stillness and peace; others involve concentrating on an object, such as a candle or flower.

- Reiki and other forms of hands-on healing use energy points (chakras) in the body to balance the mental, spiritual, emotional and physical sides of the patient. Anyone can practise Reiki and you or your child could be attuned to using it for self-healing or to use on other family members. Some people use it for the relief of pain.

'If you want to be healthy, speak truthfully to yourself, if not to other people, about your fear. Value and accept yourself. Be optimistic. Practise relaxation. Being healthy is very much a matter of attitude.'

Dorothy Rowe, *Beyond Fear*, Harper Perennial, Anniversary Reissue, 2007.

- Yoga, tai chi, breathing techniques, aromatherapy massage, Indian head massage, Bach Flower Remedies, acupuncture, or acupressure for children who don't like needles, are among the many other alternative treatments that are worthwhile investigating.

HANDLE®

HANDLE, an American Institute launched in 1994 by the late Judith Bluestone, a neurodevelopmental specialist who was herself born brain-damaged, stands for Holistic Approach to NeuroDevelopment and Learning Efficiency. HANDLE practitioners use a holistic, non-drug approach to help people with ADD, ADHD and other neurodevelopmental disorders like autism, dyslexia, Tourette's Syndrome and many more mentioned in this book. Having healed herself, Judith's mission was to help others with neurodevelopmental issues.

'My mission is to move hundreds and thousands from dysfunction to function, from despair to hope.'

Judith Bluestone
(1944-2009)

Practitioners address the root cause of the behavioural disorders they treat, preferring to overlook labels like ADHD, which they maintain are misleading. 'No one has an attention deficit. Everyone is always attending to something.' We all have attentional priorities and people who can't set and hold these for specific tasks have an attentional priority disorder (APD), they say. Practitioners believe that APD is neither hereditary nor irreversible and that tendencies are inherited.

They see behavioural symptoms as an indication of how the physical parts of the body, particularly the nervous system and brain are interacting, in the way that a headache can indicate eyestrain. Once these weaknesses have been diagnosed, HANDLE's techniques can strengthen them to reduce these behaviours.

According to HANDLE, the body-mind link reflects the effects of numerous environmental and lifestyle factors likely to affect human behaviours and they list the following:

- Chemicals.
- Allergens.
- Nutritional deficits.
- Toxins.

- Sound.

- Light.

- TV viewing.

- Video game playing.

The effects can be reversed and HANDLE prefers to regard its approach as 'a set of guiding principles . . . the body organises the brain and not the other way around'. The idea is to move people with ADHD and other neurodevelopmental disorders from dysfunction to function by making an assessment of how systems are working or not working – eyes, inner ears and how people react to environmental influences. Then gentle tailored programmes are produced from a variety of disciplines (medicine, rehabilitation, psychology, education and nutrition), so that they can be carried out at home for about 20 to 30 minutes each day to reorganise the system. Activities are not stressful and stimulate the links between the body and brain.

Among the results listed that clients can expect to see are:

- Ability to sustain auditory attention, filtering and focusing sound.

- Ability to sustain visual attention, efficient visual function.

- Increased sense of security sitting or standing or transitions.

- Decreased sensory overload.

- Decreased irritability.

- Increased ability to respond rather than react.

- Easier multi-tracking and information processing.

Alternative therapists work slowly and treatments tend to have a cumulative effect. In the Western world we are used to taking pills and expecting a quick fix, but most therapies will involve a course of treatment that may last for several visits, so you may have to persevere. Remember to talk to your doctor for professional medical advice before investigating alternative therapies.

Summing Up

Talking therapy is not a quick fix. It can take a long time and it can sometimes be disturbing. Talking therapies can help your child to discuss their issues and consider what their ADHD means to them. They can find better ways to deal with it in a safe environment, guided by someone who is not judgmental and whom they can learn to trust. Alternative therapies can have a calming effect or help alter moods to a more positive state. These can work alongside or independently of medication and talking therapies.

Chapter Seven

You Are What You Eat

The food controversy

With the obvious exception of the Ritalin debate, no guidance has courted quite so much controversy as diet and nutrition for ADHD sufferers. Those against it insist there is no research proving that diet is connected with ADHD, while those for have found that cutting out additives, preservatives and those foods to which their children may have shown an intolerance makes a noticeable difference to their symptoms. For them, the proof of the pudding is in the eating, or the not eating in this case. If it works, it may be worth a shot.

Some scientists think that food can be a trigger and they suggest that children with ADHD should try a restricted diet for a few weeks to see which foods affect their behaviour. Dutch researchers found that behaviour improved for 78% of children with ADHD who were placed on a restricted diet. When possible trigger foods were added 63% of them relapsed. They concluded that while food sensitivity played a part in ADHD, an allergic reaction didn't cause it but that dietary intervention was worth considering.

Of course it may not work for everyone, in the same way that any other treatments, traditional and alternative, don't work for everyone, for we are all individuals who react differently. It's a matter of finding what works for your child, learning as much about it as you can to ensure their safety and including it in your healing programme if you choose to do so. Eating healthily doesn't only apply to the ADHD child, it applies to your entire family and the population at large.

Let's see how this notion first came about in relation to ADHD.

The Feingold Diet

Dr Ben F. Feingold (1899-1982) was chief of allergy at Kaiser Permanente Medical Centre in San Francisco during the 1950s and 1960s. As a paediatrician and allergist, he noticed that some of his patients who were sensitive to aspirin were also sensitive to certain foods and additives. This affected them both physically and behaviourally.

In the 1960s and 1970s, Dr Feingold developed his 'KP' diet, which later became dubbed the Feingold Diet. His diet helped about 50% of his patients who were hyperactive at the time.

'Let your food be your medicine and your medicine be your food.'
Hippocrates, c.400BC.

Dr Feingold found that some plants created a chemical similar to aspirin called acetylsalicylic acid and that fruits and other foods containing it could cause sensitivity in some patients, in addition to additives. The success rate for children eliminating additives and salicylates from their diet by the 1970s rose to about 70%, although it has since been refined and is said to be producing a 90% success rate.

Salicylates

Salicylates can be found in many foods, including the following:

Berries	Paprika	Cake mixes
Peppermints	Chewing gum	Prunes
Curry powder	Puddings	Dill
Raisins	Ice cream	Seeds
Liquorice	Soft drinks	Nuts
Thyme	Oregano	Turmeric

The Feingold Association

Feingold Associations were started by support groups and now the exclusion diet can be followed by logging on to the Feingold Association's website at www.feingold.org for guidelines.

Feingold's critics

Additives are cheap to produce and foods containing them, like drugs, result in huge profits for the manufacturer. Interestingly, critics of the Feingold Diet tend to be from these industries and the early studies were conducted by them.

If the Feingold Diet does not work for everyone, this can be for a variety of reasons, often because of missed ingredients or other health issues. In these cases, the Association has further suggestions to offer. They don't claim that diet alone causes hyperactivity and admit that there are other causes. Using an exclusion diet is another option, one that seeks to eliminate some of the symptoms rather than just suppressing them.

Improved behaviour without additives

As a result of studies on three-year-olds, commissioned by the government in 2004, researchers from the University of Southampton advocated the banning of additives from food to reduce hyperactivity. Some schools in England and Wales banned additives and found improved behaviour from their pupils after two weeks, as did their parents.

However, it wasn't until 2007 that the university carried out a much bigger study into the effects of artificial food colourings and preservatives on children's behaviour, with ADHD in mind. The research was commissioned by the Food Standards Agency, which advised parents of ADHD children to avoid specific artificial colourings. When combined with the preservative sodium benzoate, these could adversely affect children's behaviour.

The European Food Safety Authority (EFSA) is currently reviewing the safety of food colours approved for use in the European Union. You may find that several big supermarkets like ASDA, Tesco, Marks & Spencer and Sainsbury's have removed some food additives from their products, as have some manufacturers.

'It's hoped that due to the success of this initiative, food manufacturers will recognise the benefit of further reducing or eliminating unnecessary colours and additives in their production methods.'

Carol Davies, schools catering manager, Conwy, Wales, BBC News 24, Wales, 6th May 2004.

What do colourings and preservatives do?

Preservatives

Preservatives are used to give foods a longer shelf life as they prevent food from going off.

- Sodium benzoate (E211) can be found in soft drinks, fizzy drinks, squashes, confectionery, ice cream, pickles, sauces, crisps and infant medicines.

- Sulphur dioxide (E220) is used on dried fruit to prevent the growth of mould or bacteria.

- Nitrite and nitrate (E249 to E252) are used to cure meats like bacon, ham or corned beef.

- Sugar, salt and vinegar also preserve some foods.

Colourings

Colours make food look more appetising when some of their normal colour fades during processing. They contain no nutritional value. The colours below were tested, together with sodium benzoate, and linked to increased hyperactivity.

'If parents are concerned about any additives, they should remember that, by law, food additives must be listed on the label so they can make the choice to avoid the product if they want to.'

Food Standards Agency, 2007.

Colourings	E Number	Foods founds in:
Allura Red	E129	Sweets, drinks, medicines.
Carmoisine	E122	Jams, sweets, sauces, yoghurts, jellies, cheesecake mixes, infant medicines.
Ponceau 4R (Cochineal Red)	E124	Dessert toppings, jelly, canned strawberries, fruit pie fillings, salami, seafood dressings, infant medicines.

Quinoline Yellow	E104	Ice creams and lollies, smoked haddock.
Sunset Yellow	E110	Orange jelly, apricot jam, hot chocolate mixes, canned fish, packet soup, infant medicines.
Tartrazine	E102	Fizzy drinks, ice cream, sweets, chewing gum, jam, yoghurt and infant medicines.

Avoiding E numbers

The Children's Food Campaign, backed by several other organisations, reacted strongly, saying that the government were not going far enough and that the Food Standards Agency should ban additives known to cause hyperactivity in children. They have since asked for further studies.

Other artificial flavourings, preservatives and thickeners are used by food manufacturers in the processing of their products. The 'E' signifies classification by the EU and some manufacturers tend to use just the additive's name to aid consumers who wish to avoid them.

Food nasties

If you have access to the Internet, visit www.netmums.com. Netmums have an informative networking site where you can find out more about the latest manufacturers to act on additives, learn which additives to avoid, which foods may be affecting your child's behaviour and can take a look at healthy foods. Look at their 'food' page and press 'food nasties' on the side panel for more information.

Essential fatty acids (EFAs)

Some studies have highlighted reduced levels of essential fatty acids (EFAs) among ADHD children, which are said to affect behaviour and learning. The body doesn't make its own EFAs and we have to obtain them in our diets. However, children with ADHD have been found to need more essential fats than normal because they don't absorb them as well as they should or convert them adequately.

- Omega-3 alpha-linolenic acid is the Omega-3 essential fat found in linseed, flaxseed, hempseed, rapeseed, pumpkin seeds and walnuts. It is converted in the body to docosahexaenoic acid (DHA) and eicosapentaenoic acid (EPA) and is also found in oily fish like salmon, tuna, herring, trout, mackerel and sardines. DHA and EPA aren't essential because the body can make its own but sometimes they are low because of difficulties with the conversion process, so they are classified as EFAs.

- Omega-6 fatty acids (linoleic acid) are found in hempseeds, sunflower seeds, pumpkin seeds and walnuts.

Essential fat deficiency symptoms

Research on EFA deficiency and hyperactivity carried out in 1981 by Sally Bunday and her mother, Vicky Colquhoun, who together founded the Hyperactive Children's Support Group (HACSG), found links with some allergic conditions in addition to zinc deficiency. Sally and her late mother spearheaded the campaign to raise awareness of nutritional deficiencies and the importance of diet among ADHD children. Sally's son was a hyperactive child treated by drugs until she eliminated additives from his diet and noticed his improvement. You can visit the HACSG website at www.hacsg.org.uk to find out more. The HACSG is Britain's leading champion of diet and hyperactivity.

Among their research findings, the following characteristics were found in children with additives in their diet:

- Excessive thirst.

- Frequent urination.

- Dry skin and hair.

- Eczema.
- Asthma.
- Other allergies.
- High percentage of males.

Daily intake

EFAs are polyunsaturated fats and they are essential to the diet. They should account for about one third of our fat intake.

The value of seeds

Seeds are an excellent source of fats, protein, vitamins and minerals. Patrick Holford, nutritional therapist, recommends a heaped tablespoon of seeds a day made up of half flaxseeds and half sesame, sunflower, hemp and pumpkin seeds. It's best to grind them in a coffee grinder, as some can be hard to chew and may pass through the system undigested. You can sprinkle them on the family's breakfast cereal or add them to soups, salads and casseroles. Make sure you store them in a tightly sealed glass jar in the fridge.

Holford also recommends using cold pressed seed oils as salad dressings and as a substitute for butter. Oil blends or flaxseed oil are recommended but should not be used for frying or in hot food.

Jeannine Virtue, an American freelance journalist and mother of an ADHD son, has been a champion of better diet and nutrition for ADHD children for years. Jeannine runs a support service for parents on the Internet and provides some great ideas for using flax oil in food, loads of tips on storing and buying it and meal ideas, like yoghurt smoothies with flax oil and using flax oil instead of sugar and ice cream. You can check this out at www.add-adhd-help-center. com. Jeannine has also produced a book of recipes for ADHD children's meals and this can be downloaded free from her site. Lack of space prevents me from reproducing some of them here, but it's certainly worth visiting for yourself.

EFA supplements

Although our diet is the most sensible way of getting EFAs, supplements can also be taken but, as with any supplement, this should be after consultation with a qualified nutritional therapist who will work out the correct amount your child should take and recommend a reputable brand.

The cheapest brands are not necessarily the best and some supplements contain the sort of additives ADHD children need to avoid, so it's important not to self-treat. Your therapist will tell you where to obtain them, usually by mail order or from the Nutricentre in London where all the major makes are stocked under one roof.

The Nutricentre, which was taken over by Tesco some years ago, is worth a visit. They have a large bookstore on alternative health issues and consulting rooms for alternative therapists at the Hale Clinic (this is on the floor above the Nutricentre). You can send for their catalogue and check out their other UK outlets on their website. (See the help list for further information.)

It can take a few months for EFAs to get into your child's system. If no difference is seen in their behaviour by then, EFA deficiency may not be the problem.

Gluten sensitivity and coeliac disease

Links have been found between coeliac disease and ADHD symptoms by Israeli and Italian researchers. A gluten-free diet was found to be effective among patients. Gluten, a type of protein, can be found in rye, barley, wheat and wheat products, such as bread, pasta, breakfast cereals and many other manufactured products. Avoiding gluten altogether is the antidote, as there is no other treatment or cure for coeliac disease, which is an autoimmune response to gluten.

Nowadays, many food manufacturers produce gluten-free products and supermarkets and health food shops sell wide ranges of them. Care needs to be taken with possible cross-contamination of gluten-free foods, particularly in restaurants where the same equipment, such as toasters, are used for wheat bread and gluten free.

There are tests available on the NHS for coeliac disease, such as blood tests and biopsy but it is hard to diagnose, particularly as some sufferers may experience no symptoms and test results are not always accurate. Coeliac disease can take many years to develop and is often misdiagnosed as irritable bowel syndrome (IBS). Some people who react to gluten products may have gluten intolerance but are not necessarily coeliac.

It is thought that drugs prescribed for ADHD may mask what are coeliac or gluten sensitivity neurological symptoms.

Coeliac UK is a source of valuable information, including a food and drink directory, gluten-free products and services, gluten-free recipes and background to coeliac disease.

Other food supplements

It's a good idea to include some other nutrients in your child's diet and these can also be obtained as supplements. Here are some that are thought to be lacking in ADHD children. However, before using supplements it is essential to first consult a qualified nutritional therapist to obtain a proper assessment and nutritional programme.

Vitamins/Minerals	Function	Foods found in:
Amino Acids	Derived from protein foods, used to make neurotransmitters and enzymes needed by the brain.	Good quality proteins like lean meat, fish, eggs, dairy products, beans, lentils, nuts, seeds.
Vitamin B Complex (many B vitamins)	Healthy nervous system.	Dark green vegetables, sunflower seeds, nuts, wholegrains.
Vitamin C (ascorbic acid)	Good for the immune system.	Citrus fruits, tomatoes, potatoes, broccoli, green peppers.

Zinc (trace element)	Important for immunity to disease.	Shellfish, meat, poultry, eggs, a little in grains.
Chromium (trace element)	For balancing blood sugar and maintaining blood cholesterol levels.	Meat, wholegrains, lentils, spices.
Magnesium (works with calcium)	For healthy bones and muscles and blood sugar control.	Dark green vegetables.

Nutritionist or dietician?

Confusion surrounds the difference between a dietician, who you are likely to see under the NHS, and a nutritional therapist, who you would pay to see privately.

For more information on this, the Nutrition Society published a Department of Health briefing note in 2004 called 'Understanding the differences between nutrition health professionals', which can be accessed by visiting www.nutritionsociety.org.

The British Association for Applied Nutrition & Nutritional Therapy (BANT) also explains the difference at www.bant.org.uk – simply click on 'general information' and then 'nutrition titles' for more information. A brief summary is given below.

The differences explained

Dieticians – work for the NHS. Regulated by the Health Professions Council. Members of the British Dietetic Association.

■ Devise eating plans for medical conditions.

■ Promote good health through diet for individuals, groups and communities.

Nutritionists – usually work in the food industry, research or academia in government or other agencies.

- Informational rather than therapeutic.

Nutritional therapists – meet standards of the National Occupational Standards for Nutritional Therapy and are regulated by the Nutritional Therapy Council. Diet and lifestyle advice to help ailments and promote optimal health.

- Advise patients on natural detox.

- Colon health.

- Digestion and absorption.

- Use of supplements.

- Use tests and questionnaires to assist diagnosis and treatments.

- Treat patients who haven't responded to traditional medicine.

- Parents of children with learning and behavioural issues consult them.

- Must be fully qualified and hold full professional indemnity insurance.

You can also search for a practitioner in your area on BANT's website.

Food and chemical intolerances

Nutritional therapists are trained in dealing with food intolerances and may suggest eliminating key triggers from your child's diet, such as:

- Wheat (and/or other gluten products).

- Dairy products.

- Yeast.

- Sugars.

- Individual foods to which they may react adversely.

Some alternatives

- Rice, oat and soya milks.

- Non-gluten and wheat-free products, such as non-gluten cereals and flour, rice cakes, rice pasta.

- Yeast-free stock cubes.

- Synthetic sweeteners like saccharine or aspartame are not recommended but many products are now sweetened with apple juice.

- Organic produce.

Cooking without . . .

Cooking without some of the products that have been a part of your diet for most of your life can sound ominous. However, there are several cookery books on the market that specialise in alternative ingredients, such as nutritional therapist Erica White's *Beat Candida Cookbook* or Barbara Cousins' *Cooking Without, Cooking Without Made Easy* and *Vegetarian Cooking Without*. (See the book list for further details.)

Make your home smell nice safely

Smelly chemical sprays and some chemical cleaning products affect some children and are best avoided. Natural aromatherapy oils can be used in the bath, in a burner or mixed with water and sprayed in your home. Journalist Janey Lee Grace's book, *Imperfectly Natural Woman* is full of information on sources of natural chemical-free products.

Summing Up

It doesn't take a genius to realise that whatever you put into your body will be instrumental in renewing and maintaining the cells and organs that keep you healthy, alive and functioning. If some of those substances that you and your family eat, touch or inhale don't agree with you, then it makes sense to avoid them. However, in doing so you need to be careful that your family are well nourished. With the right information about alternative foods and proper professional guidance, you can help your child and benefit the whole family at the same time with a new and healthier way of eating and living.

Chapter Eight

Support From Your School

All schools are legally obliged to identify pupils who have educational or behavioural difficulties and can make a referral to CAMHS for a special needs assessment. During the assessment, the school and teachers will be asked for their opinions. The school's SENCO will answer questionnaires and individual teachers will be asked for their comments about your child's behaviour. (See chapter 3 for more information.)

If you are at all concerned about your child, it's best to talk first to their teacher or the school's SENCO. If you can work in co-operation with the school, it will make life easier for all concerned. Your child's opinions should also be included if possible.

Is it hard to get help?

If your school disagrees that your child should have a referral for an assessment to obtain a Statement of Special Educational Needs for special support, you can apply for one yourself by contacting your local education authority's (LEA) SEN section.

Some authorities are not so helpful and parents complain that teachers are not trained in how to deal with ADHD, some believing more in punishment for poor behaviour rather than understanding it and employing appropriate strategies.

You may find that lack of finance for ADHD support is preventing your child from receiving appropriate help. Although LEAs receive extra money for special needs pupils, some parents claim that the government is running a postcode lottery and that whether you receive any support depends on which local authority you live in. This appears to have led to some parents taking the drastic step of moving to another area where appropriate funding is made available.

Get it in writing

If your child's school complains about their behaviour, it's vital that you get something in writing from the school to say what the problem is. This record can be handed to your medical team as proof, for it is not uncommon for parents to be wrongly accused of using their child's behaviour to apply for disability allowances. It's important to keep copies of all correspondence relating to your child's situation at school and a diary of incidents.

'According to the Office of National Statistics, children with hyperkinetic disorder are 11 times more likely to be excluded than other children.'

Moving forwards

If teachers know that your child has been diagnosed with ADHD, they can take the appropriate action to move forwards.

Discipline and behaviour policies

Details of school discipline and behaviour policies can be found at www.direct.gov.uk under 'parents', together with details about fixed period and permanent exclusions.

Policies may have some differences elsewhere and some issues have been devolved by the government to the National Assembly for Wales, the Scottish Parliament and the Northern Ireland Assembly. Links to these sites can be found on the DirectGov website (see the help list).

Exclusions

If your child has not been diagnosed with ADHD, you may be contacted by the school frequently because of behavioural problems in class or during play. Your child may even be excluded several times, but this should only occur as a last resort when all else has failed. Non-permanent exclusions are limited to a maximum of 45 school days in one year and the school should first call you, then write to you giving reasons for why this has happened.

If you're concerned, make an appointment to see the teacher, SENCO or head teacher and go armed with the questions that you want to ask. Remember to take any medical reports that you would like them to see.

Complaints procedures

If you find that the school is not being co-operative, contact your local Parent Partnership Scheme (the school should give you details) or the Independent Panel for Special Education Advice (IPSEA). If you live in Scotland, contact the Independent Special Education Advice (ISEA) and in Northern Ireland, Special Educational Needs Advice Centre (SENAC). If all else fails, you can go through the formal complaints procedure.

Your child's rights

The Education Act 1981, states that when children find learning more difficult than most children in the same age group, they have special educational needs. It includes children who have mental, physical or behavioural difficulties and recommends that they are educated in mainstream schools with the provision of extra support. The SEN Code of Practice gives the main guidance (see page 92.)

The Education Act 1996, gives the definition of special educational needs (SEN) and refers to those children who experience learning difficulties that necessitate special educational provision.

Scotland

The Scottish Parliament passed new legislation under the Additional Support for Learning (Scotland) Act 2004, changing some of the 1984 Act. See below for details:

▓ Special educational needs was replaced by additional support needs.

- Provision is no longer outlined in the Record of Needs.

- The criteria for additional support needs is no longer confined to children with a disability.

- Co-ordinated support plans were instituted.

- Requests can be made for all children or young people who have additional support needs.

- New Mediation, Dispute Resolution and Tribunal Services were implemented.

- The legal rights of parents, children and young people were altered.

Northern Ireland

'I studied the children and they taught me how to teach them.'

Maria Montessori, Italian-born educator (1870-1952).

The Education (Northern Ireland) Order 1996, amended by the Special Educational Needs and Disability (Northern Ireland) Order 2005, applies. It is similar to England and Wales and states that statutory responsibility for securing provision for special educational needs children lies with the Education and Library Boards and Boards of Governors of mainstream schools.

Getting help

The role of the SENCO

The school's special educational needs co-ordinator is referred to as the SENCO or INCO (inclusion co-ordinator). Depending on the size of your school, this may be a teacher, a team, the head or deputy teacher. (Scottish schools have special educational needs advisers.) The SENCO will act under the following circumstances:

- If your child isn't moving forwards.

- If they aren't developing skills.

- If they are displaying poor behaviour that isn't responding to the help available.

- If they are finding it hard to communicate with their peers and teachers and have speech or language needs.

The role of the teacher

Some education authorities are very helpful and produce brochures explaining ADHD or take an active role in local support groups. Books and videos about ADHD are also available among special needs resources for teachers.

ADHD children can easily be distracted by what is going on around them in the classroom, can lose concentration easily and can find it hard to sit still and listen attentively. There are many strategies that can be employed by teachers to help combat some of these behavioural tendencies.

A few basic tips that are widely recommended are shown below.

Ten tips for teachers

- ADD children tend to gaze out of the window often, so placing them away from windows and nearer to you at the front of the class is a better option.

- Make sure your classroom rules are clear and easy to understand.

- Make the ADHD children monitors or give them special jobs to do, so that other pupils will view them positively.

- Let them come to the board and write words on it.

- Be specific about any directions for tasks to be done. Have a checklist for every subject and give out homework task charts.

- Ask the child to say out loud what they have to do, then to repeat it silently to themselves.

- Try to vary activities so that pupils aren't doing the same thing all the time. Have some sitting down tasks and alternate them with more physical activities, so they can't get bored easily.

- Give them specific tasks to carry out with goals to achieve and rewards for achieving them.

'The student with ADHD is likely to have difficulties with the learning style supported by the school system – that of being a good listener, being able to sit and focus for extended periods of time and of having good reading and oral language skills.'

Philippa Greathead, speech language pathologist, Speech Language Learning Centre, Westmead, NSW, Australia.

- In books, large fonts will help them to focus but avoid texts with illustrations that don't relate to the task in the text. Try not to include too many activities on one page.

- Rewards for good behaviour and plenty of praise will help to raise their self-esteem.

SEN Code of Practice

You can download a copy of the current Code of Practice for England, which came into effect in January 2002, from the Department for Education website, www.education.gov.uk. Search for SEN Code of Practice. Bilingual copies of the Welsh code are also available, as is a good parents' guide. Scotland's code contains different procedures and a supplement to Northern Ireland's code became effective on 1st September 2005. Copies of both documents can be downloaded or applied for from their Department of Education website (see the help list for further information.)

The Code of Practice outlines the duties of LEAs and schools regarding the identification and assessment of SEN pupils. It differs from the old 1994 Code of Practice in that it considers the effects of the original legislation and introduces some new rights and duties.

There are time limits within which the LEA must decide on whether to allow an assessment. The code stipulates that the process must be done in 26 weeks.

- Request considered   6 weeks

- Assessment and decision   10 weeks

- Drafting statement   2 weeks

- Finalisation   8 weeks

SEN statements could soon be a thing of the past. The government's Achievement for All scheme, originally launched by the Labour government in 2009, intends to issue single assessments in their place that cover children's education, health and social care needs until they reach 25. It is also expected that parents will have the legal right to control funding of their child's support costs by 2014.

An Ofsted report in 2010 revealed that about 450,000 children on the register had been inaccurately diagnosed and the planned move should cut down the numbers on the SEN register by about 10%.

It means that School Action and School Action Plus will be scrapped and that teachers will train to help children who don't need such strong support. It is hoped to cut out the waiting time for equipment and other local services that currently exists. Voluntary groups and parents will also have more involvement in the process.

Individual Education Plan (IEP)

As special needs children are usually educated in mainstream schools, all teachers need to be able to handle special needs pupils. For pupils having difficulties, some teachers, in discussion with the SENCOs, draw up an Individual Education Plan (IEP). This includes:

- Targets.
- Actions.
- Help from parents.
- Outcome.

Make sure you are consulted and kept in the picture.

School Action (or Early Years Action)

The SENCO will monitor progress and suggest special equipment like computers or special learning materials that might help.

School Action Plus (or Early Years Action Plus)

If School Action isn't working, the SENCO may feel it necessary to bring in outside specialist support, like an educational psychologist or speech and language therapist.

If that fails, they may then approach the LEA and ask for a statutory assessment for a Statement of Special Educational Needs, specifying what help the school can give your child.

Statement of Special Educational Needs

Only about 3% of children are considered to need this. If your child is one of them, after the assessment the LEA must produce a statement which states your child's needs and the help they require from your school, backed by the LEA. This will be reviewed every year and you will be able to attend the meetings.

You will be given 15 days to check over the draft statement and reply. You need to have evidence from the assessments for any additions you may wish to make.

What happens if the support isn't adequate?

If you're not happy with the support that you get from your school, or if the school doesn't honour the statement, you need to find out the reasons for this at school. It may simply be a matter of staff shortages or something that can be dealt with and sorted out.

■ If you are not happy about the school's response, but agree with the statement, you need to contact sen.queries@dcsf.gsi.gov.

■ If you don't agree with the provisions in the statement, you can ask for a reassessment.

■ If you still don't agree with the amended statement or are refused a reassessment, you can lodge an appeal with the SEN and Disability Tribunal (SENDIST).

What if the statement is refused?

If the LEA decides that a Statement of Special Educational Needs isn't appropriate for your child, they must tell you this in writing. A note in lieu will describe your child's special educational and non-educational needs and recommend appropriate support. You should also be given reasons why the LEA has refused a statement.

A copy will be sent to your child's school, unless you indicate otherwise. The information in the assessment reports should be helpful to the school in planning your child's support but the note in lieu isn't a legally binding document.

If you're unhappy about this, you can go for mediation or you can appeal.

The right to appeal

You have the right to appeal against their decision to the SENDIST, an independent organisation that deals with parents' appeals against their LEAs on statutory assessments and statements.

You can also appeal if:

- The LEA refuses to carry out an assessment.

- If you disagree with any of the provisions on a statement.

- If they refuse to reassess an existing statement.

- If they stop your child's statement.

The tribunal is composed of a chairman (a lawyer) and two members with experience of special educational needs. You will be able to ask two people who know your child well to speak on your behalf at the hearing. You can go there alone or take with you a member of a parents' group or voluntary organisation.

'The word education must not be understood in the sense of teaching but of assisting the psychological development of the child.'
Maria Montessori.

National Parent Partnership Services

Parent Partnership Services are impartial and are there to give support and information to parents of special needs children. If you need support for a tribunal, they will advise you and guide you through the process. The Parent Partnership Officer can also introduce you to other local organisations.

Summing Up

If you can work together with the school amicably, it should make things easier for everyone. This isn't always the case and trying to obtain assessments and statements isn't easy. It often boils down to finance and there can be a long waiting period for applications. However, in the meantime, teachers can take positive action in the classroom. There are systems in place for support for parents and the right to appeal if necessary. It's important to keep records of incidents, phone conversations and meetings, together with copies of all correspondence relating to your child's education and application for special needs support.

For more information, see *Special Educational Needs – A Parent's Guide* (Need2Know).

Chapter Nine

Family Support

Understanding ADHD, its symptoms and treatment, and the sort of support that you can expect to find, is essential to helping your child. It's hard enough trying to cope with a hyperactive child and any other siblings, as well as all the other responsibilities that caring for a family entails, without feeling lost and helpless to know where to turn.

However, at least you will be armed with the facts. These days, research findings, books, videos and DVDs about ADHD are readily available, not to mention the wealth of material on the Internet. In addition, ADHD support groups have sprung up all over the country.

What do support groups have to offer?

According to ADDept, the Yorkshire ADHD and Learning Ability Support Group, there are currently 350 ADHD support groups in the UK. Support groups have invariably been set up by parents of ADHD children; some of these parents may even have ADHD themselves. Some have the support of their LEAs, like Flintshire, and many are registered charities run by volunteers.

Some support groups are localised and others are national organisations. Their websites contain a huge amount of information on ADHD and hidden disabilities, and lots of links to other sites. There are also other benefits, including:

- Regular newsletters.
- Factsheets.
- Telephone helplines.
- Advocacy and mediation services.

- Benefits information.
- Monthly meetings.
- Outreach work.
- Drop-in facilities.

It's worth checking to see if you have one in your area. It will take some of the isolation out of your situation; there may be meetings you can attend and you may feel like volunteering to help in some way.

If there isn't a support group in your area, you may feel that you would like to start one of your own. But how would you go about it?

'If there isn't a support group in your area, you may feel that you would like to start one of your own. But how would you go about it?'

Setting up a support group

- Attend an existing support group to find out how it works and chat to the organisers. Ask for some tips on setting up your group.

- Try to find some volunteers to help you. Ask friends, relatives and at school. You could put a notice on the board at school or in your local library.

- Decide on a specific role for each volunteer and hold a meeting to decide on what needs to be done.

    - Where will your group meet?

    - What are your goals?

    - What sort of age group are you aiming to attract – parents, teenagers, families? Decide on one and work towards setting up your support group for them.

    - How will you finance the group and what is your budget?

    - How often will you hold meetings?

    - What time will you meet and for how long?

    - What about materials and supplies?

    - How will you make yourselves known?

    - What will your group be called?

- Display postcards at school, in the library, medical centre, supermarket, newsagent's window and anywhere else with a noticeboard that will give you permission.

- Try to get your local paper to give you some editorial announcing the group and send them regular press releases. Press releases are simply information sheets containing the answers to the 5 Ws: who, what, why, when and where. Try to confine them to one A4 sheet, double spaced. Include the group's name and logo (if you have one) at the top and contact details at the bottom, together with the date. To begin with, you could call in to your local newspaper office and introduce yourself; have a chat with whoever is manning the newsdesk or the editor, if possible, and leave your contact details.

- Draw up some information sheets containing your contact details and an itinerary for the first (and subsequent) meeting to hand out to visitors.

- Set up a network of volunteers who don't mind giving out their phone numbers and email addresses to people that want to contact them for support or information.

- Invite some speakers who can talk about ADHD and/or other related issues.

- Set up a website containing details of meetings, ADHD information and contact details. If you don't know how to do this yourself and you can't afford to pay a web designer, you can buy a ready-made site template and follow the easy instructions to build a professional-looking site quite quickly, like Mr Site, 0844 414 5158, or from most computer shops. You can buy a Takeaway Mr Site boxed version for beginners for £24.99, standard version for £39.99 or a website pro version for £99.99. Details at www.mrsite.com.

- Your support group may take a while to take off, so don't be discouraged if the numbers are few to begin with. Word will need to get around, so persevere.

A useful support organisation to get in touch with is Contact A Family, which gives advice, information and support to parents of disabled children, regardless of their disability or health condition. They can put families in contact with each other, locally and nationally – every year they reach about 275,000 families. Their website gives advice on setting up and running a support group. Information packs include information on setting up a website. Details can be found at www.cafamily.org.uk.

National ADHD Awareness Week

Launched in 2006 by ADDISS and the 22 support groups in its Affiliation Network, this has now become an annual event, usually held around September. Its aims are given as:

- Improving the understanding of ADHD children's behaviour and acceptance of their needs.
- Better access to resources and support for ADHD children and their families.
- More focus within the school system to make sure that the government's pledge that 'Every Child Matters' includes ADHD children.

'Behaviour management programmes are becoming popular so that parents can create and maintain a more structured environment in the home.'

The role of the parent

It's important to manage your child's behaviour in your home to prevent the atmosphere from descending into chaos. Everyone else in the home is bound to be affected, so it's in everyone's interest to understand how to engage with your child to their best advantage. Behaviour management programmes are becoming popular so that parents can create and maintain a more structured environment in the home. A positive attitude, praise and encouragement play a big part in this kind of training.

ABC behaviour management skills

Using the ABC analysis, you will find out how to alter your child's behaviour and how important it is to praise them when they behave well. The earlier you begin this technique, the earlier they will learn, although it isn't always easy to identify toddlers with ADHD. It is said to work well for children with oppositional behaviour problems connected with ADHD, so that bad behaviour can be prevented before it escalates and good behaviour encouraged.

- **A**ntecedents – look for triggers that spark off their bad behaviour; it's important to recognise what caused it.
- **B**ehaviour – what exactly did your child do or not do and how long did it last?

■ **C**onsequences – how did it affect other people and what happened to your child as a result?

Parenting training

Normal parenting probably isn't going to have any effect on your child if they have behavioural problems, so it's worth investigating what would be involved in a parent training programme.

You will learn:

■ Different ways of dealing with your child's difficult behaviour.

■ To make eye contact when addressing them.

■ To establish clear rules.

■ To give any instructions in one sentence only, so that it's easier to remember.

■ To give punishments for poor behaviour on the spot rather than waiting until a later time.

■ To give your child rewards for when they have behaved well or have achieved something.

■ To be lavish with praise and to ensure your child can hear you when you mention their achievement to others.

■ To take a positive view of your child and the way they behave.

■ To keep calm so your own attitude doesn't affect your child's behaviour. Take two steps back and think about what you're going to say before you do so. This will give you a chance to calm down.

■ To find a special 'quiet' place for your child to sit in until they've calmed down.

■ To develop and maintain a regular structured routine using lists or charts to remind your child.

■ To make time to play with your child, varying the activity to keep them engaged.

1-2-3 Magic

Packed with easy parenting techniques for children aged 2 to 12, a book that many parents find helpful is Thomas Phelan's *1-2-3 Magic: Effective Discipline for Children*. It suggests three simple steps to get quick results.

- Step 1: Control Obnoxious Behaviour is designed to stop your child being awkward and doing things that you don't want them to do.

- Step 2: Encourage Good Behaviour suggests methods to get your child doing what you want them to do.

- Step 3: Strengthen Relationships helps to reinforce your bond with your child.

Other techniques include testing and manipulation, handling misbehaviour in public and avoiding the Talk-Persuade-Argue-Yell-Hit syndrome. A similar title for teachers, *1-2-3 Magic for Teachers*, suggests effective classroom disciplines and includes methods for communicating productively with parents.

Support group ADDISS run excellent 1-2-3 Magic courses for schools and for parents and carers in effective discipline for children aged 2 to 12.

They offer training courses for people working in education, parents and carers, adults and young people and the community. 'We train practitioners on our behaviour management programmes. It gets to the heart of the problem very quickly and helps worn out parents,' said Andrea Bilbow, ADDISS's founder.

'65% of parents of ADHD children have divorced, separated or experienced marital distress as a result of their child's/children's condition.'

ADDISS Families Survey, 2006.

Family therapy

Some specialists feel that treating the whole family is the best way to ensure a positive atmosphere in the home that will be helpful to your child, although research into its effectiveness is limited. Family therapy can help to alleviate the pressures in your home, especially if your child's behaviour is affecting siblings or other family members. ADHD symptoms can also be triggered by what happens in the family.

Systemic therapy works on the principle that if one family member changes then the rest will automatically follow. Therapists try to discover what causes problems in the family before deciding on what changes to make. Sessions may take place every month or less and a clinical psychologist carries out the therapy.

Support from social services

Many families have benefitted from help provided by social services, but there are also many who view the service with alarm. Reports tend to be mixed but social workers should be able to assist you with Disability Living Allowance (DLA) claims or finding facilities to help you and your child.

In 2002, a survey of UK social workers revealed that over a third of childcare social workers knew little about stimulant medication used to treat ADHD. It was also felt that they should have more training in this area. In the Trent region, consultations with parents of ADHD children revealed that they felt they were the best co-ordinators of care for their own children. They mentioned the difficulties in obtaining support from social services, which included DLA and respite care.

If you have social workers on your case, you can check to see if they are registered in the Register of Social Workers on the General Social Care Council's website (see the help list.) You will also find their Code of Conduct and legal information there. Links to registers for Scotland, Wales and Northern Ireland are on the site.

All local authorities, and any other services with which you are involved, are required to work to Every Child Matters, the government programme linking up children's services (www.everychildmatters.gov.uk). Local authorities should have a 'no secrets' policy for the Protection of Vulnerable Adults, Domestic Violence and Child Protection. Make sure you check that your social workers know about this and have read the policy.

'If you have social workers on your case, you can check to see if they are registered in the Register of Social Workers on the General Social Care Council's website.'

According to an ADDISS Families Survey carried out in 2006, 79% of parents said that neither they nor their ADHD child had been offered any help from social services, despite 15% of parents having lost their jobs because they had to care for their child and 48% suffering from depression because of the impact ADHD had on their families.

Disability Living Allowance (DLA)

One familiar accusation levelled at parents of ADHD children, usually made by deniers of ADHD, is that they use ADHD as an excuse to claim benefits. However, Disability Living Allowance is claimed for children, not for parents. You are entitled to claim if your child needs more looking after than others of the same age; you can claim for DLA if your child has a physical or mental disability or both and if the disability is severe enough for them to need help. A medical examination is not usually needed.

Disability Living Allowance is a tax-free benefit and is divided into two components. Some people may be eligible for one component, others may receive both of them.

- Care component (higher, middle, lower). This is for looking after your child's needs and how much you need to supervise them.

- Mobility component (higher, lower). You can claim if your child needs help getting about.

If you get DLA, it may increase the amount of other benefits you are entitled to.

How to make a claim

You can claim online or apply for a claim pack for children under the age of 16.

- Phone the Benefit Enquiry Line, a confidential freephone service for disabled people and carers: 0800 88 22 00. The line is open from 8.30am to 6.30pm, Monday to Friday.

- Contact your local Jobcentre Plus office or local social security office, or

- Download the form from the website at www.direct.gov.uk and fill it in at home, or

- Download a claim form to complete on your computer.

- To claim online, go to www.dwp.gov.uk/eservice.

Carer's Allowance

Carer's allowances are available for people who help someone who is disabled. Claims are handled by the Carer's Allowance Unit in Preston (see the help list). They can send you a claim form in English or in Welsh.

You can claim if you spend at least 35 hours a week looking after someone who receives an Attendance Allowance or Disability Living Allowance at the middle or high rate for personal care. Details and application forms for a carer's allowance can also be downloaded from the same website. To claim online, go to www.dwp.gov.uk/carersallowance.

Summing Up

Trying to keep the family on an even keel by learning strategies to cope with your ADHD child's behaviour is a must if you are to establish and maintain a good balance and a pleasant atmosphere in your home. Using instant punishments and rewards and displaying a positive attitude will do much for your child's self-esteem but, above all, bringing about change for the positive may go some way to controlling their behavioural patterns and making life easier for everyone. Joining or starting a support group will prevent you from feeling isolated and will provide you with information and contacts who can empathise and understand your situation.

Chapter Ten

Transition to Adulthood

Some children overcome their ADHD by the time they grow up but for about 60% their symptoms will continue into adolescence and adulthood.

Making the transition is one area where some parents feel that not enough support is available and that teachers and social services are simply not geared to either recognising the symptoms of ADHD or understanding how to react to an ADHD child.

Adolescence is a difficult time for most children, and the additional stress of coping with ADHD symptoms that they can't control can result in a downhill spiral of depression, anxiety and low self-esteem. They may have problems finding jobs and participating in social activities. Some may also end up on the wrong side of the law or become addicted to drugs or alcohol, in which case the Youth and Criminal Justice System may be involved.

The wrong side of the law

The British Medical Association claims that because ADHD and hidden disabilities are not assessed and diagnosed in care homes, national crime figures have risen. They say these children account for 23% of all crime, with 48% owing to medical disorders and other mental health conditions relating to ADHD. Around 20% of those in Feltham Young Offenders Institute are said to have behavioural problems like ADHD.

ADDept Yorkshire comment that a recent study showed that 75% of prison inmates have hidden disabilities and that, although the government is slowly recognising this, most of them are still not receiving treatment because the necessary resources are not available.

What is a Transition Plan?

Your local authority (LA) is required to put together a Transition Plan in Year 9 when your child is 14. (Education authority (EA) in Scotland and Boards in Northern Ireland.)

In England, Connexions will deliver the plan and in Wales, Careers Wales. Your head teacher should write to you about the first Transition Plan review meeting, or the LA if your child is not going to school. You should also receive a copy of any written reports at least two weeks before the meeting and a copy of the plan once it is finalised.

Who must attend the review meeting?

- Parents and carers (parents on equal footing with professionals).
- Teacher(s).
- A representative from the LA.
- Social services.
- Health professionals involved in your child's care.
- A representative from the Connexions service or Careers Wales.
- Any others considered to be relevant by the head teacher.

Any recorded reviews of your child must also be taken to the meeting.

The plan follows targets set at the previous annual review of your child's SEN statement.

What if there is no Statement of Special Educational Needs?

In 1998, children with SEN statements amounted to 36,200 but by 2004 this figure had fallen to 26,000 and in 2006 to 22,600. The total number of children assessed for SEN statements dropped from 37,340 in 1997 to 23,770 in 2006. (Source: 1997-2001 figures: http://www.dfes.gov.uk/rsgateway/DB/SBU/b000301/sb12-2001.pdf Table 2; 2001-2007 figures: http://www.dfes.gov.uk/rsgateway/DB/SFR/s000732/sfr20_2007_tables_oh.xls Table 1a) In 2005, over a million children with special needs had no statements. It is impossible to know how many ADHD children have statements because many are lumped together with children suffering from the autistic spectrum. About a third of cases heard by the SEN Tribunal now concern children with behavioural and emotional disorders (the category under which ADHD falls) and autism. (Source: *The Guardian*, 6th December 2005.)

If your child isn't statemented and has ADHD, they still need additional support for their transition. Connexions is required to ensure that all young people with difficulties have a written report drawn up showing their needs for further education and training and how they can be met. It isn't compulsory for children on School Action or School Action Plus to have a Transition Plan but it's advisable. If your child has no statement, it's a good idea to contact Connexions or Careers Wales to arrange a meeting yourself. The final plan will be given to your child's new educational or training provider.

What you may need for the meeting

Because you know your child better than anyone and you will have records of all the professionals who have been involved in their care, it's a good idea to list them all and take any records and written information involving them to the meeting.

Put together evidence of any achievements your child may have made in or out of school and a list of their talents and interests. This could reflect on the sort of courses that might be available or that they intend to follow.

After the meeting

Your child's head teacher must ensure that the plan is drawn up and Connexions or Careers Wales must action it. The LA has to make the recommended services available to your child during the transition period and annual review meetings must take place until they leave the school.

Further Annual Transition Plan meetings

Every year until your child is 18, further review meetings should take place to see if the plan is still relevant to your child's needs or if it needs adjusting. Your school should arrange these. When your child is 16 (Year 11), social services should discuss any planning meetings needed with the adult care manager. If your child is leaving school, a Learning and Skills Plan has to be drawn up, detailing any further education. The LA should also apply for funding from the Learning and Skills Council in England or the Welsh Assembly.

The adult care team

Your child will finally be transferred to the adult care team when they reach 18, although it can sometimes happen earlier or later. When they leave the world of education altogether, they will be covered by the Disabled Persons Act and can still be supported by Connexions or Careers Wales until they reach 25 years of age.

The Disabled Persons Act

Social Care decide whether your child can be defined as 'disabled' and you should receive notification of this decision in writing. If your child's ADHD is not recognised as a disablement, then you may challenge it.

How is disablement defined?

The Disabled Persons Act classifies a child as disabled if they are blind, deaf, dumb, suffering from a mental disorder or substantially and permanently handicapped by illness, injury, congenital deformity or other such disability as may be prescribed. That includes children with:

- Physical or mental disability.

- Chronic sickness.

- Sensory disability.

- Mental illness.

- Communication impairment.

It's recommended that you register your child as disabled in case you need evidence for those who may deny this. It is becoming increasingly common for education providers to deny ADHD as a disability. However, teachers have no qualifications to make such a diagnosis. It's worth remembering too that ADHD is covered by the Disability Discrimination Act.

Further and higher education

Around the time your child is about 15, it's a good idea to consider which educational establishment they might attend and to visit some of them. The Transition Plan should help your child to understand what is available to them, but they should also visit any college they're thinking of applying to, go to open days and check out their support facilities.

Universities and colleges usually have an equalities office and a disability/ learning support co-ordinator. You can ask for copies of their disability statements.

In the meantime, there are various possibilities for your child to consider, including further and higher education, specialist colleges or acquiring job-based skills. The website www.NetDoctor.co.uk has some excellent factsheets containing tips on both study and work for people with ADHD which are full of advice and contact information.

If your child wishes to go straight into work, Jobcentre Plus is a useful source of information and support for disabled people and Careers Wales gives advice and guidance.

'Once your child is over 18 and thinking about going into employment, it might be a good idea for them to find a job where they can work from home.'

Adults at work

Once your child is over 18 and thinking about going into employment, it might be a good idea for them to find a job where they can work from home. Many companies allow employees to do this nowadays and keep in touch by phone, email and teleconferencing. If they do work in company premises, suggest that they ask for their own office so that they aren't distracted by their colleagues around them.

But first they have to find a job. If they've continued into higher education, their careers counsellors will help them and the national newspapers carry advertisements for graduates. Local Jobcentres have disability employment advisers with details of access to work and there are several good job search sites on the Internet. It makes sense to look for something to match the skills and qualifications they already have or something that suits their interests.

Research spread over 10 countries has revealed that adults with ADHD work 22 days less a year than people who don't have ADHD. The research was undertaken for the World Health Organisation World Mental Health Survey. The ADHD workers – both self-employed and employed – took off an average of eight days a year. They did less work during 21 days and poor quality work over 13 days, which added up to a half day of lost work. Although workplace screening programmes and treatment were suggested, ADHD expert Professor Philip Asherson from London's Institute of Psychiatry said in a BBC interview that this could lead to stigmatisation and that adults with ADHD should be included in general health screens by GPs or occupational health departments.

Tips for easier working

- Working to deadlines will keep them focused. Keeping a diary and 'to do lists' each day will help to prevent forgetfulness or missed meetings.

- If unsure about instructions, it's always best to ask the speaker to explain more clearly or to repeat what they've said but, better still, try to get them in writing.

- When boredom with a task sets in, it's a good idea to turn to something else for a while and go back to any dull tasks when feeling more motivated.

- If faced with big tasks that might seem daunting, it's easier to tackle them a bit at a time rather than the whole lot at once.

- Turning off the phone or using earphones to cut out distracting noises can be helpful.

- Taking short breaks can help to focus attention.

- If things become too difficult, talking to the boss or human resources manager about any problems may result in some workable solutions.

- Working flexitime can also be useful.

'I seldom think about my limitations and they never make me sad. Perhaps there is just a touch of yearning at times but it is vague, like a breeze among flowers.'

Helen Keller (1880-1968), deaf-blind American writer.

Adults with ADHD

Many adults do not know that they have ADHD or that their behaviour and difficulty with social interactions is due to what is classified as a hidden impairment. ADHD, together with any co-morbidities, can make their lives and those of the people around them intolerable. Some adults may only find out that their symptoms are ADHD-related if their own child is diagnosed with it, and some symptoms become less obvious as an adult matures. You may recognise some of them here.

Some possible symptoms

- Do you lose your temper easily?
- Do you create awkward situations and atmospheres because of your violent actions and reactions?
- Are you restless and fidgety?
- Do you act on impulse without thinking first?
- Do you find it hard to concentrate for long and have a short attention span?
- Do you start to do things then lose interest and move on to something else without finishing what you started?
- Do you tend to exasperate people?
- Do you lack organisational skills?

Diagnosing adults with ADHD

If you suspect that you have ADHD, then you should see your doctor about it. However, because of a dearth of research into adult ADHD, doctors may not recognise ADHD symptoms, and co-morbid conditions are likely to make a diagnosis more difficult. The criteria for diagnosing ADHD was developed for children, so psychiatric rating scales relating to questions are used to determine if adults are likely to have ADHD.

- The Wender Utah Scale is the scale most often used. It consists of 61 questions concerning your childhood symptoms; persistent hyperactivity and inattention are the two main criteria plus two of five others. Other conditions also need to be ruled out.

- The Brown Attention-Activation Disorder Scale (40 questions).

- The Copeland Symptom Checklist for Adult ADD (63 questions based on emotional, cognitive and social symptoms).

- Triolo's Attention-Deficit Scales for Adults.

- Conner's Adult ADHD Rating Scales.

Treatment for ADHD adults

Treatment for adults is similar to that for children, invariably a combination of medication and talking therapies, or therapy alone if drugs aren't considered appropriate. Stimulants and antidepressants are mainly used with Ritalin as the main medication. If this is ineffective or you have an intolerance, NICE recommend switching to atomoxetine or dexamfetamines.

Summing Up

Many children with ADHD continue into adolescence and adulthood with this hidden impairment. Support is available for them to make the transition but not all parents find this as helpful as they would like, particularly in the cases where professionals deny the existence of ADHD or disagree with their child's diagnosis. Some professionals may not have received training in how to help children with ADHD and a lack of understanding can lead to some attitudes being misunderstood as offending behaviour. Being aware of legislation and your child's rights will help you to fight their corner if you have to and keeping copies of all correspondence and reports is essential. Try to learn as much as you can about this stage of your child's development and how to encourage them with their ongoing education and job searches. Self-help for adults with ADHD includes regular routines, talking to others with the condition, coping with stress and gaining the support of family and friends.

Help List

ADD/ADHD Help Centre

709-2 Plaza Drive #105, Chesterton, Indiana 46304, USA
support@add-adhd-help-center.com
www.add-adhd-help-center.com
Provides a large amount of articles on various aspects of ADHD and a book of
free recipes to download.

ADDept (Yorkshire AD/HD and Learning Ability Support Group)

30 The Paddock, York, YO26 6AW
Tel: 01904 782556
mark-breen@mindless.com
Provides support for parents and children with ADHD and hidden disabilities.
Campaigns for specialist services, organises training for professionals and
public and social activities. Open 24 hours, every day.

ADDISS

Premier House, 112 Station Road, Edgware, Middlesex, HA8 7BJ
Tel: 020 8952 2800
info@addiss.co.uk
www.addiss.co.uk
Provides information, training and support for parents, sufferers and
professionals in ADHD and related learning and behavioural difficulties.
ADDISS has a resource centre of books and videos and a reference library
containing articles.

ADD Resources

223 Tacoma Ave S #100, Tacoma WA 98402, USA
www.addresources.org
Provides 100 free articles about ADHD and links to related websites.

Asperger's Syndrome Foundation

Finsbury Square Charity Centre, Royal London House, Suite 5A,
1st Floor, 22-25 Finsbury Square, London EC2A 1DX
info@aspergerfoundation.org.uk
www.aspergerfoundation.org.uk
This is a small registered charity committed to promoting awareness and understanding of Asperger's syndrome. Fundraising, seminars and information sheets.

British Association for Applied Nutrition and Nutritional Therapy (BANT)

27 Old Gloucester Street, London, WC1N 3XX
Tel: 08706 061284
theadministrator@bant.org.uk
www.bant.org.uk
The professional association for nutritional therapists. Visit the website to find a BANT practitioner in your area.

British Association for Counselling and Psychotherapy

BACP House, 15 St John's Business Park, Lutterworth, Leicestershire, LE17 4HB
Tel: 01455 883300
bacp@bacp.co.uk
www.bacp.co.uk
This professional association advises schools on setting up counselling services, assists the NHS on service provision, works with voluntary agencies and supports independent practitioners. Find a therapist on their website.

British Dyslexia Association

Unit 8 Bracknell Beeches, Old Bracknell Lane, Bracknell, RG12 7BW
Helpline: 0845 251 9002
Tel: 0845 251 9003 (office)
helpline@bdadyslexia.org.uk
www.bdadyslexia.org.uk
Helps with early ID and support in schools for dyslexic pupils and school leavers in higher education and the workplace. Aims to influence the government and other institutions.

British Homeopathic Association

Hahnemann House, 29 Park Street West, Luton, LU1 3BE
Tel: 01582 408675
www.britishhomeopathic.org
info@britishhomeopathic.org
Provides information on medical homeopathy for the public and registered health-care professionals. Find a practitioner, articles and information.

Careers Wales

Tel: 0800 100 900 (Learn Direct)
www.careerswales.com
Provides careers information and advice for young people and adults in Wales. Careers centres and shops open all year.

Carer's Allowance Unit

Palatine House, Lancaster Road, Preston, PR1 1NS
Tel: 0845 608 4321
cau.customer-services@dwp.gsi.gov.uk
www.dwp.gov.uk
www.direct.gov.uk/en/DisabledPeople/index.htm
Visit the Department for Work and Pensions website for more information.

Clare Jones, BA (Hons) Dip ION mBANT (Nutritional Therapy)

164 Manchester Road, Manchester M16 0DZ
Tel: 07985 166606
info@clarejones-nutrition.co.uk
www.clarejones-nutrition.co.uk
Manchester-based private nutritional therapist treating a variety of conditions.

Coeliac UK

3rd Floor, Apollo Centre, Desborough Road, High Wycombe, Bucks HP11 2QW
Tel: 01494 437278; Helpline 0845 305 2060
www.coeliac.org.uk
Scotland Offices:
1 St Colme Street, Edinburgh EH3 6AA
0131 220 8342

Communicative And Supportive Teaching/Learning Environment (CASTLE),

Scholefield Road, London N19 3ES
Tel and Fax: 020 7686 2405
marion@hyndamn.demon.co.uk
Recognises HANDLE in the UK. 'Not being able to talk doesn't mean you have nothing to say'

Connexions

Tel: 0808 001 3219; texts: 0776 641 3219
www.directgov.uk
From April 2011, Connexions Direct moved to the Directgov online site, giving online information, advice and support for young people. The Next Step service deals with careers for youth and adults and young people can still contact advisers for careers, work and learning advice. Advisers available 8am-2am, 7 days.

Contact a Family

209-211 City Road, London, EC1V 1JN
Tel: 020 7608 8700
Helpline: 0808 808 3555
Email: helpline@cafamily.org.uk
www.cafamily.org.uk
Provides support, advice and information for families with disabled children or specific conditions. Puts parents of ADHD children and others in touch with similar families and gives advice on how to set up support groups. Factsheets on relevant topics are available.

Department for Education

Castle View House, East Lane, Runcorn, Cheshire, WA7 2GJ
Tel: 0370 000 2288
www.education.gov.uk/
Useful information for parents and young people. www.direct.gov.uk

Department of Health

The FSA is no longer responsible for nutrition in England and Wales: call Department of Health customer service centre: 0207 210 4850. The Department of Health is responsible for nutrition policy, including nutrition labelling, in England.

Department of Health for Northern Ireland

Castle Buildings, Stormont Estate, Belfast, BT4 3SQ
Tel: 028 90520500
www.dhsspsni.gov.uk
mail@deni.gov.uk
Provides information on health, social services and safety in Northern Ireland. Visit the publications section for more information.

DfES Publications

Head Office:
PO Box 5050, Sherwood Park, Annesley, Nottinghamshire, NG15 ODJ
Order line: 0845 60 222 60
dfes@prolog.uk.com
www.dfes.gov.uk
The SEN Code of Practice is obtainable for free by email or from the website.
Wales:
Welsh Government, Cathays Park, Cardiff Bay, CF10 3NQ
Tel: 0845 010 3300 (English) or 0845 010 4400 (Welsh)
www.wales.gov.uk
Bilingual copies of the Welsh code are available from the website.
Scotland:
Tel: 08457 741 741
ceu@scotland.gsi.gov.uk
www.scotland.gov.uk
Contact the Scottish department for Scotland's code.
Northern Ireland:
Rathgael House, Balloo Road, Rathgill, Bangor, BT19 7PR
Tel: (NI) 028 9127 9279
www.deni.gov.uk
Contact the Northern Ireland department for their code.

DirectGov

www.direct.gov.uk
The Central Office of Information site produces a huge range of information from UK government departments, ranging from special educational needs to local NHS services. Browse by topic (e.g. education) or by audience groups (e.g. disabled people or parents). Links for advice and support are also provided. The government has devolved some issues to the Northern Ireland Assembly, the Scottish Parliament and the National Assembly for Wales. Links to their websites can be found on this site.

Disability Benefits Unit

Warbreck House, Warbreck Hill Road, Blackpool, FY2 0YE
Tel: 0800 88 22 00 (Benefit Enquiry Line)
Tel: 08457 123 456 (Disability Living Allowance & Attendance Allowance)
Carer's Allowance Unit: 0845 608 4321
BEL-Customer-Services@dwp.gsi.gov.uk

Dyslexia Action

Park House, Wick Road, Egham, Surrey, TW20 0HH
Tel: 01784 222300
info@dyslexiaaction.org.uk
www.dyslexiaaction.org.uk
Provides information and support on dyslexia and literacy difficulties. Assessment, tuition and training of dyslexia teachers is available. Visit the website for contact details of centres in England, Wales and Scotland.

Educational Grants Services (EGS)

Family Action, 501-505 Kingsland Road, London E8 4AU
Tel: 0207 241 7459
Email: egas.enquiry@family-action.org.uk
www.family-action.org.uk/
Run by the Family Welfare Association, EGAS provides advice and guidance on funding for students in post-16 education and training in the UK. Download a guide to student funding.

Equality and Human Rights Commission (formerly Disability Rights Commission)

Helpline:
England: 0845 604 6610
Wales: 0845 604 8810
Scotland: 0845 604 5510
www.equalityhumanrights.com
This commission champions equality and human rights, works to eliminate discrimination, reduce inequality, protect human rights and ensures that everyone has a fair chance to participate in society. Has offices in Manchester, London, Glasgow and Cardiff.

Family Lives

CAN Mezzanine, 49-51 East Road, London N1 6AH
Tel: 0207 553 3080
Helpline: 0808 800 2222
http://familylives.org.uk/
24-hour Parentline for help with family issues. Run face-to-groups and work in schools, GP surgeries and prisons.

Feingold Association of the United States

37 Shell Road, 2nd Floor, Rocky Point, NY 11778
help@feingold.org
www.feingold.org
This website is devoted to the Feingold Diet programme. It includes background information, newsletters, success stories, FAQs, lists of research papers published in peer-reviewed journals and guidance on how to apply for details of the diet.

General Social Care Council

Myson House, Railway Terrace, Rugby CV21 3HT
Tel: 01788 572119; 0845 070 0630
www.gscc.org.uk
Check the register for social workers, codes of practice and legal information.

The HANDLE® institute

7 Mount Lassen Drive, Suite B-110, San Rafael, CA 94903
Tel: (415) 479-1800
Fax: (415) 230-4695
support@handle.org
www.handle.org
Its Mission Statement is 'to provide an effective alternative for diagnosing and treating neurodevelopmental disorders across the lifespan to individuals, organisations and communities, through research, education, professional training and clinical services'. See the website for practitioners in England, Wales and Ireland.

Certified HANDLE Practitioner and Instructor and European Regional Education Director for The HANDLE Institute.

Cathy Stingley
20 Northfield Way, Brighton, E Sussex BN2 8EH
01273 5584545
www.thoughtfultherapies.com
handleofhomer@yahoo.com

Hi2u 4 people with hidden impairments

www.hi2u.org.uk
www.adhd.org.uk (section on ADHD)
An informative website for people with ADHD, Asperger's syndrome, dyslexia and other neurological differences and hidden impairments. It contains links to articles, tips on management of ADHD, treatments and a list of support groups.

Healthcare Improvement Scotland (NHS QIS)

Edinburgh:
Elliott House, 8-10 Hillside Crescent, Edinburgh, EH7 5EA
Tel: 0131 623 4300
Glasgow:
Delta House, 50 West Nile Street, Glasgow, G1 2NP
Tel: 0141 225 6999
comments@nhshealthquality.org
www.nhshealthquality.org

Set up to improve quality of care and treatment delivered by NHS Scotland.

The Hyperactive Children's Support Group

71 Whyke Lane, Chichester, West Sussex, PO19 7PD
Tel: 01243 539966
hacsg@hacsg.org.uk
www.hacsg.org.uk
Support for ADHD children and families. Favours the dietary and nutritional approach to hyperactivity and has conducted essential research into the effects of colourings and preservatives on ADHD children.

IMAGEN Project

Brain and Body Centre, University of Nottingham, University Park, Nottingham, NG7 2RD
imagen@nottingham.ac.uk
www.imagen-info.com
A European research project investigating mental health and risk-taking behaviour in teenagers.

Independent Panel for Special Education Advice (IPSEA)

ipsea.info@ipsea.org.uk
www.ipsea.org.uk
Free and independent advice for parents of children with special educational needs, including appealing to the Special Educational Needs and Disability Tribunal. Special Educational Needs and Disability Tribunal Appeal or Claim: 01394 384 711. Free monthly advice sessions for parents of children with ADHD at CAB, Saffron Walden, Essex. For appointments, tel: 01799 582030.

Independent Special Education Advice (ISEA) Scotland

164 High Street, Dalkeith, Midlothian, Scotland, EH22 1AY
Tel: 0131 454 0096
isea@isea.org.uk
www.isea.org.uk
Established by parents to provide free, independent advice and information.

Jobcentre Plus

www.jobcentreplus.gov.uk
Part of the Department for Work and Pensions. Helps with employment, searching for work and provides extra support via disability employment advisers. Impact assessments and action plans for work, publications, equality schemes and access to work scheme.

Learn Direct

FREEPOST learndirect
Tel: 0800 101 901, 7am-11pm, 7 days a week
Learners in Scotland:
Tel: 0808 100 9000
Post-16 learning in England and Wales; provides careers advice, online learning centres for improving IT, Maths and English and work-based
e-learning courses.

Liverpool Adult ADHD Ladders of Life Support Group

West Everton Community Council, 33 Everton Brow, L3 8PU
Teresa Fitzgerald, 0779 8585 656; Shirley Hand, 0782 6004 436
www.adhdliverpool.com
Helps people with ADHD/Asperger's achieve their full potential through education and support. Every Thursday: Parents 10.00am-12.00pm; ADHD Adults 1.00-3.00pm.

Lothian Adult ADHD service

Royal Edinburgh Hospital, Morningside Terrace, Edinburgh EH10 5HF
Tel: 0131 537 6000
Email: premal.shah@nhslothian.scot.nhs.uk
Contact: Dr Prem Shah
Scotland's first dedicated ADHD outpatient service for adults. Provides advice, education, assessments and treatments. Referrals by GPs or psychiatrists in Lothian regions but outside referrals considered.

Mental Health Foundation

London:
9th Floor, Sea Containers House, 20 Upper Ground, London, SE1 9QB

Tel: 020 7803 1101

mhf@mhf.org.uk

Glasgow:

Merchants House, 30 George Square, Glasgow, G2 1EG

Tel: 0141 572 0125

scotland@mhf.org.uk

www.mentalhealth.org.uk

Information on mental health problems and learning disabilities.

Wales:

Merlin House, 1 Langstone Business Park, Priory Drive, Newport NP18 2HJ

Tel: 01633 415 434

MIND (National Association for Mental Health)

15-19 Broadway, London, E15 4BQ

Tel: 0208 519 2122

www.mind.org.uk

email: contact@mind.org.uk

Mind Infoline: PO Box 277, Manchester M60 3XN

0300 123 3393

info@mind.org.uk

www.mind.org.uk

Mind Cymru

3rd Floor, Quebec House, Castlebridge, 5-19 Cowbridge Road East, Cardiff, CF11 9AB

Tel: 02920 395 123

contactwales@mind.org.uk

www.mind.org.uk

There are around 200 local MIND associations in England and Wales. Search for your local branch onsite. MIND campaigns for equal rights and challenges discrimination and other services for those with mental health needs. The website includes lots of information and free factsheets.

National Council of Psychotherapists

PO Box 7219, Heanor, DE75 9AG

Tel: 0845 230 6072

http://www.ncphq.co.uk/
ncphq@btinternet.com
This is a national association of mainly private therapists. Use the website to search for a psychotherapist in your area.

National Institute for Clinical Excellence (NICE)

MidCity Place, 71 High Holborn, London, WC1V 6NA
Tel: 0845 003 7780
nice@nice.org.uk
www.nice.org.uk
Provides national guidance on promoting good health and preventing and treating ill health. Guidelines available for patients on the use of medication for ADHD.

National Parent Partnership Network

8 Wakely Street, London, EC1V 7QE
Tel: 0207 843 6058
www.parentpartnership.org.uk
Supports parents and carers of children with special educational needs.
The website contains information on how to contact local parent partnership organisations. Information and publications also available.

www.NetDoctor.co.uk

This website deals with a comprehensive range of complaints. It gives advice and tip lists for teachers and parents of children with ADHD and explains statutory assessments, SEN statements and legal rights. Information on ongoing education and ADHD in the workplace is also provided.

www.netmums.com

124 Mildred Avenue, Watford, WD18 7DX
contactus@netmums.com
A family of local websites set up and run by mums. Campaigns include 'Stop Pushing Junk Food to Our Children' and 'Teenagers and Knives'. Provides local information on education, childcare, community, social and employment issues. There are 155 local netmums sites and more to follow.

NHS Direct

Tel: 0845 4647 (24 hour helpline)
www.nhsdirect.nhs.uk
Informative NHS health website allowing you to search for a local health service.
Website also provides information on common health questions, including ADHD, a
self-help guide and health encyclopaedia.

Niamh Mental Wellbeing

Central Office, 80 University Street, Belfast, BT7 1HE
Tel: 028 9032 8474
paul-barton@btconnect.com
http://www.niamhwellbeing.org/Contact-Us-4850.html
A range of services for people with mental health needs. Has 14 Beacon Centres
across Northern Ireland providing support, social activities, outreach, alternative
therapies, education and discussions.

Northern Ireland ADHD Support Centre (NI-ADD)

86 Eglantine Avenue, Belfast, BT9 6EW
Tel: 028 9020 0110
hello@addni.net
www.ni-add.org.uk
A presentation on the 'Implications for Teachers of ADHD' is available on the
website. Their aims are 'supporting and empowering children, parents and young
adults with AD/HD'. Valuable information on ADHD is provided.

The Nutricentre

Unit 3, Kendal Court, Kendal Avenue, London, W3 0RU
Tel: 020 7436 5122
enq@nutricentre.com
www.nutricentre.com
The largest alternative health dispensary in Europe; other outlets at listed Tesco
stores.

Patrick Holford

Holford & Associates Ltd, PO Box 53979, London, SW15 6TZ
Tel: 0208 789 1040

Email: admin@patrickholford.com
www.patrickholford.com
Provides information on nutritional therapy and healthy eating.

Teacher Net

Tel: 0870 000 2288
info@dcsf.gsi.gov.uk
www.education.gov.uk/schools
The government's education site for teachers. Contains useful information for parents and carers.

The Royal College of Psychiatrists

17 Belgrave Square, London, SW1X 8PG
Tel: 020 7235 2351 (ext 259 for leaflets)
rcpsych@rcpsych.ac.uk
www.rcpsych.ac.uk
Provides up-to-date information on current mental health issues and is a good source for leaflets on mental health topics, including ADHD.

The School Food Trust

3rd Floor, 2 St Paul's Place, 125 Norfolk Street, Sheffield, S1 2JF
Tel: 0114 274 2318
info@schoolfoodtrust.org.uk
www.schoolfoodtrust.org.uk
Set up in 2005 by the Department for Education and Skills (DfES) to improve the quality of school meals and standards. Provides advice and information.

Scottish Association for Mental Health

Brunswick House, 51 Wilson Street, Glasgow G1 1UZ
Tel: 0141 530 1000
Email: info@samh.org.uk
www.samh.org.uk
Supports people with mental health problems and other forms of social exclusion. Campaigns to influence policy and improve care services in Scotland. Committed to the principles of recovery and user involvement.

Scottish Intercollegiate Guidelines Network (SIGN Executive)

Elliott House, 8-10 Hillside Crescent, Edinburgh, EH7 5EA
Tel: 0131 6234720
www.sign.ac.uk
Email: duncan.service@nhs.net
SIGN work to improve patient healthcare in Scotland by creating national clinical guidelines. Patient guidelines can be downloaded for free.

SEN Teacher

site@senteacher.org
www.senteacher.org
SEN Teacher provides cost-free teaching and learning resources for students with special needs and learning disabilities. All the resources available or listed here are free for use in schools, colleges and at home.

SENAC (Northern Ireland)

Graham House, Knockbracken Healthcare Park, Saintfield Road, Belfast,
BT8 8BH
Tel: 028 9079 5779
info@senac.co.uk
www.senac.co.uk
Provides assistance for parents appealing Board decisions to the SEN Tribunal.

Skill

Head Office:
Chapter House, 18-20 Crucifix Lane, London, SE1 3JW
Tel: 0800 328 5050
info@skill.org.uk
www.skill.org.uk
Skill Northern Ireland:
North Derby Street Industrial Estate, Belfast, BT15 3HN
Tel: 028 9028 7000
admin@skillni.org.uk
Skill Scotland:
Norton Park, 57 Albion Road, Edinburgh, EH7 5QY
Tel: 0131 475 2348

admin@skillscotland.org.uk

Skill Wales:

Suite 14, 2nd Floor, The Executive Centre, Temple Court, Cathedral Road, Cardiff, CF11 9HA

Tel: 02920 786506

temp@skillwales.org.uk

National Bureau for Students with Disabilities – promotes opportunities for young people and adults with any kind of impairment in post-16 education, training and employment.

Skills Funding Agency

Cheylesmore House, Quinton Road, Coventry, CV1 2WT

Telephone: 0845 377 5000

Email: info@skillsfundingagency.bis.gov.uk

http://skillsfundingagency.bis.gov.uk/

Young People's Learning Agency

Tel: 0800 121 8989 9am-5pm

Email: MFT-EMA@skillsfundingagency.bis.gov.uk

Professional and Career Development Loans (PCDL) tel Next Steps 0800 100 900. http://www.ypla.gov.uk/

Special Educational Needs and Disability Tribunal (SENDIST)

Darlington:

2nd Floor Old Hall, Mowden Hall, Staindrop Road, Darlington, DL3 9BG

SEN & DDA Tel: 01325 392760

Email: sendistqueries@tribunals.gsi.gov.uk

www.sendist.gov.uk

Wales:

Unit 32, Ddole Road, Enterprise Park, Llandridnod Wells, Powys, LD1 6PF

Tel: 01597 829 800

http://wales.gov.uk/sentwsub/home/?lang=en

Information and advice for parents appealing against LEA decisions of special needs assessments and statements. It includes forms, guidance, hearings and decisions, rules and legislation. New appeals for England to be sent to Darlington.

UK Council for Psychotherapy

2nd Floor, Edward House, 2 Wakley Street, London, EC1V 7LT
Tel: 020 7014 9955
info@ukcp.org.uk
www.psychotherapy.org.uk
An umbrella organisation for psychotherapy groups.

Welsh Assembly Government

Tel: 0300 0603300 or 0845 010 3300;
Welsh: 0300 0604400 or 0845 010 4400
Email: wag-en@mailuk.custhelp.com
www.wales.gov.uk
Funds, plans and promotes post-16 education and training in Wales (excluding higher education).

YoungMinds

Suite 11, Baden Place, Crosby Row, London, SE1 1YW
Tel: 020 7089 5050
Parents' helpline: 0808 802 5544
www.youngminds.org.uk
A national charity committed to improving the mental health of children and young people under 25. Provides information on child mental health issues, advice, training and campaigns.

Sources of further information

ADDISS Information Centre, www.addiss.co.uk.

'Additives in Food', Food and Drink Federation, 20 Feb 2008, www.fdf.org.uk/additives.aspx.

'ADHD and hyperkinetic disorder: for parents and teachers, Factsheet 5: Mental Health and Growing Up', www.rcpsych.ac.uk.

ADHD information from the Mental Health Foundation, www.mhf.org.uk.

'ADHD: SEN Teacher – Teaching resources (co-morbid conditions)', www.senteacher.org.

'ADHD – Services Over Scotland', Report of the service profiling exercise, NHS Quality Improvement Scotland, March 2007.

'ADHD: What Causes ADHD?', www.netdoktor.com.

'Agency revises advice on certain artificial colours', Food Standards Agency, 11 September 2007, www.food.gov.uk/news/newsarchive/2007/sep/foodcolours.

American Academy of Sleep Medicine. 'Sleep loss in early childhood may contribute to the development of ADHD symptoms'. ScienceDaily, 15 June 2011. Web 28 Jun 2011.

Asherson, Dr P MRCPsych, PhD, 'Adult ADHD: How adults are affected by ADHD and what can be done about it', BBC, Science & Nature, *Horizon*: 'Living with ADHD', www.bbc.co.uk.

'Attention-Deficit/Hyperactivity Disorder' (Hyperkinetic Disorders), PsychNet-UK, www.psychnet-uk.com.

'Attention deficit and hyperkinetic disorders in children and young people', (2001), Scottish Intercollegiate Guidelines Network (SIGN), *SIGN Publication No 52*, www.sign.ac.uk.

'Attention deficit hyperactivity disorder (ADHD) in children', factsheets, BUPA, http://hcd2.bupa.co.uk.

'Attention deficit hyperactivity disorder: diagnosis and management of ADHD in children, young people and adults', NICE, *SCOPE*, www.nice.org.uk/guidelinesmanual.

Bluestone, J and Suliteanu, M C, 'ADHD retrospective outcome study', OTR Judith Bluestone's remarks at the NIH ADHD Consensus Conference in 1998.

Borrill, Dr J, 'All About ADHD', Mental Health Foundation booklet – *Alternative approaches for children with ADHD*, April 2000, www.mhf.org.uk.

Bunday, Sally, 'Additives and Mood in ADHD', Foods Matter, www.foodsmatter.com.

Champion, G, 'Ritalin prescription fears raised', *BBC News*, Scotland, http://news.bbc.co.uk.

Chan, E MD, MPH, 'The role of Complementary and Alternative Medicine in Attention-Deficit Hyperactivity Disorder'. Division of General Pediatrics, Children's Hospital, Boston, Massachusetts. J Dev Behav Pediatr 23:S37–S45, 2002.

'Characteristics of Gifted/Creative Children', The National Foundation for Gifted and Creative Children, www.nfgcc.org.

Clegg, J, Harshorne, M, 'Speech and language therapy in hyperactivity: a United Kingdom perspective in complex cases', Human Communication Sciences, University of Sheffield, Sheffield, United Kingdom.

Coghill, Dr D, (reviewed by), 'Cognitive Behaviour Therapy, (how can it help ADHD?)', www.netdoktor.com.

Colquhon, I and Bunday, S, 'A lack of essential fats as a possible cause of hyperactivity in children', *Medical Hypotheses*, 1981, Vol 7, pp 673-9.

Contact a Family Factsheet: 'Preparing for adult life and transition', www.cafamily.org.uk.

de Graaf, R, Kessler, R C, et al, 'The prevalence and effects of Adult Attention-Deficit/hyperactivity Disorder (ADHD) on the performance of workers: Results from the WHO World Mental Health Survey Initiative', Occup Environ Med 2008;Published Online First: 27 May 2008.

Diagnostic and Statistical Manual of Mental Disorders (DSM-1V), 4th ed., American Psychiatric Association (1994), Washington DC.

Information on flaxseeds and flax oil from Jeannine Virtue, www.add-adhd-help-center.com.

'Food additives and bad behaviour', 'Food additives to avoid', www.netmums.com.

Greenhead, P, 'Language Disorders and Attention Deficit Hyperactivity Disorder', www.addiss.co.uk/languagedisorders.htm.

Health encyclopaedia – 'Attention deficit hyperactivity disorder', www.nhsdirect.nhs.uk.

'Health: Ritalin', Lords *Hansard* Text for 14 November 2007.

'How to Start a Support Group', About.com ADD/ADHD, www.add.about.com.

International Statistical Classification of Diseases and Related Health Problems, 10th Rev (ICD-10), WHO, Geneva.

'Kids on Pills' Transcript, *BBC Panorama*, April 10 2000, http://news.bbc.co.uk.

Lee, S S, Humphreys, K L, Flory, K, Liu, R, Glass, K, 'Prospective Association of Childhood Attention-deficit/hyperactivity Disorder (ADHD) and Substance Use and Abuse/Dependence: A Meta-Analytic Review', Clinical Psychology Review, 2011.

Liddle, E B, Hollis, C, et al, 'Task-related Default Mode Network modulation and inhibitory control in ADHD: effects of motivation and methylphenidate.' Journal of Child Psychology and Psychiatry, Vol 52, Issue 7, pps 761-771, July 2011.

Majorek, M, Tuchelmann T, Heusser P, 'Therapeutic Eurythmy-movement therapy for children with attention deficit hyperactivity disorder (ADHD): a pilot study', Talstrasse 381, 4204 Himmelried, Switzerland.

'Medications available in the UK', information guide, ADD/ADHD Lincolnshire Support Group: *Medication*, http://beehive.thisislincolnshire.co.uk.

'Methylphenidate, atomoxetine and dexamfetamine for attention deficit hyperactivity disorder (ADHD) in children and adolescents, understanding NICE guidance – information for children and adolescents with ADHD, their families and carers, and the public,' NHS National Institute for Health and Clinical Excellence, Information about Technology Appraisal 98, March 2006, www.nice.org.uk.

Monastra VJ, 'Electroencephalographic biofeedback (neurotherapy) as a treatment for attention deficit hyperactivity disorder: rationale and empirical foundation', FPI Attention Disorders Clinic, 2102 East Main St, Endicott, NY 13760, USA, Am J Nurs, 1975 May, Vol 75(5): pp 797-803.

Munden, A, Arcelus, J, *The AD/HD Handbook: a guide for parents and professionals on AD/HD*, Jessica Kingsley, London, 2000.

Myttas, Dr N, 'Understanding and recognising ADHD', *Practice Nursing*, 2001, Vol 12, No 7, pp278-280 and at www.addiss.co.uk/understandingadhd.htm.

'New Study Suggests Pediatric Ritalin Use May Affect Developing Brain', 19 July 2007, www.medicalnewstoday.com/articles.

News from The Hyperactive Children's Support Group, nutrition information, research into food additives and aspartame, www.hacsg.org.uk.

Niederhofer H, Pittschieler K, 'A Preliminary Investigation of ADHD symptoms in Persons with Celiac Disease', Journal of Attention Disorders, 2006 Nov; 10(2):200-4.

'Note in Lieu and Final Statement', Parent Partnership Service, Westfield Middle School, Bedford, www.bedfordshire.gov.uk/parentp.

Panorama: 'ADHD drugs have "no beneficial effects"', *BBC One News*, 12 November 2007, www.bbc.co.uk & www.bbc.co.uk/blogs.

Peisser, Dr L, Frankena PhD, K, Toorman MD, J, Savelkoul, PhD, Prof H, F, Dubois MD, Prof A E, Pereira MD, R R and others, 'Effects of a Restricted Elimination Diet on the Behaviour of Children with Attention-deficit Hyperactivity disorder' (NCA Study): a randomised controlled trial, The Lancet, Feb 5, 2011, Vol 377, No 9764, pps 494-503.

'Positive Behaviour Management Strategies + Help Sheet 3' includes general behaviour management strategies and specific interventions for individual pupils, including the ABC of behaviour management, by Linda Evans, author SENCO Week, October 2007. Can be viewed and downloaded at www.teachingexpertise.com/e-bulletins/behaviour-management-strategies-2137.

Richardson, Alexandra J, 'Fatty Acids in Dyslexia, Dyspraxia and ADHD: Can Nutrition Help?', *Food and Behaviour Research*, 2002, www.fabresearch.org.

'Ritalin', House of Commons, *Hansard*, (House of Commons Daily Debates), 12 July 2007, www.parliament.uk.

'SCIE research briefing 5: Short breaks (respite care) for children with learning disabilities', April 2004, (updated April 2005).

'SCIE research briefing 8: Attention deficit hyperactivity disorder (ADHD): how it is treated,' August 2004 (updated August 2005). www.scie.org.uk/publications/briefings.

Selikowitz, M. *ADHD the facts*, OUP, Oxford, 2004. 'Special Educational Needs Code of Practice', Nov 2001, Ref DfES/581/2001.

Selnick N MD et al, 'Range of Neurologic Disorders in Patients with Celiac Disease', Pediatrics Vol 113 No 6 June 2004

Setlik MD, J, Randall Bond, G, Ho, M, 'Adolescent Prescription ADHD Medication Abuse is Rising Along With Prescriptions for these Medications', Pediatrics, Vol 124, No 3, September 1, 2009. pps 875-880.

'Special Educational Needs (SEN), A Guide for Parents and Carers', Sept 2001, Ref Dfes/0800/2001, Department for Education and Skills, www.dfes.gov.uk.

'Special Educational Needs – what does it mean?', Appeals and Complaints, www.teachernet.gov.uk.

'The Restless and excitable child: for parents and teachers, Factsheet 1', *Mental Health and Growing Up*, 3rd Edition, www.rcpsych.ac.uk.

'Understanding the differences between nutrition health professionals: Optimum Nutrition', Briefing Note, British Association for Nutritional Therapy, March 2006, www.bant.org.uk.

'United Nations' Warnings on Ritalin', United Nations Information Service *INCB Annual Report 1995*, 28 February 1996, www.pbs.org.

Williams, N M, Zaharieva, I, et al, 'Rare chromosomal deletions and duplications in attention-deficit hyperactivity disorder: a genome-wide analysis', Lancet, Vol 376, Issue 9750. pps 1401-1408. 23 October, 2010.

Zaccheo, D, 'What is coaching?', www.addiss.co.uk.
By Erica White, Thorsons, London, 2nd Rev Ed, 1999, £14.99.
, £21.95.

Book List

1-2-3 Magic: Effective Discipline for Children 2-12 (Advice on Parenting)
By Thomas Phelan, ParentMagic Inc, 2010. £4.64.

1-2-3 Magic for Teachers: Effective Classroom Disciplines Pre-K Through Grade 8
By Thomas Phelan and Sarah Jane Shonour, Child Management Inc, USA, 2004, £12.50.

The AD/HD Handbook: a guide for parents and professionals on AD/HD
By Alison Munden and Jon Arcelus, Jessica Kingsley Publishers Ltd, London, 1999, 2000, £11.95.

Attention Deficit/Hyperactivity Disorder: A Practical Guide for Teachers (Resource Materials for Teachers)
By Paul Cooper and Katherine M Bilton, David Fulton Publishers 2002. £23.99.

ADHD Recognition Reality and Resolution
By Dr Geoffrey Kewley, Australian Council for Educational Research (ACER), 2001, £32.50.

ADHD the facts
By Mark Selikowitz, OUP, Oxford, 2009, £12.99.

Adult AD/HD: A Reader Friendly Guide to Identifying, Understanding, and Treating Adult Attention Deficit/Hyperactivity Disorder
By Thomas Whiteman, Tom Whiteman, Michele Novotni and Randy Petersen, NavPress, 2003, £8.99.

All About ADHD
By Dr Jo Borrill, Mental Health Foundation, free download at www.mentalhealth.org.uk.

Coeliac Disease: The Essential Guide
By Kate Coxon, Need2Know Books 2010, £9.99

Cooking Without
By Barbara Cousins, Thorsons, London, 2nd Rev Ed, 2000, £12.99.

Cooking Without Made Easy: Recipes free from added gluten, sugar, yeast and dairy produce
By Barbara Cousins, Harper Thorsons, London, 2005, £10.99.

Driven to Distraction: Recognizing and Coping with Attention Deficit Disorder from Childhood Through Adulthood
By Edward M Hallowell and Dr John J Ratey, Pantheon Books, 1994, Touchstone, 1995, £9.99.

Dyslexia and Other Learning Difficulties – A Parent's Guide
By Maria Chivers, Need2Know, Peterborough, 2004, £8.99.

Erica White's Beat Candida Cookbook: over 250 recipes with a 4-point plan for attacking candidiasis
By Erica White, Thorsons, London, 2nd Rev Ed, 1999, £14.99

The Feingold Cookbook for the Hyperactive Child
By Ben F. Feingold and Helene Feingold, Random House, USA, 1979, £21.95.

Hyperactive Children: A practical guide for parents
(A practical workbook containing coping strategies)
By Joanne Barton and Ronnie Russell, The Child and Family Trust, Glasgow, 1999, £18.50.

I would if I could: a teenager's guide to ADHD and hyperactivity
By Michael Gordon, Atlantic Books, London, 1991, (GSI Publications, New York, 1992), £13.95.

Hyperactive Children: A practical guide for parents
(A practical workbook containing coping strategies)
By Joanne Barton and Ronnie Russell, The Child and Family Trust, Glasgow, 1999, £18.50.

I would if I could: a teenager's guide to ADHD and hyperactivity
By Michael Gordon, Atlantic Books, London, 1991, (GSI Publications, New York, 1992), £13.95.

Imperfectly Natural Woman – getting life right the natural way
By Janey Lee Grace, Crown House Publishing Ltd, Carmarthen, 2005, £12.99.

The Left-hander's Handbook: How to Succeed in a Right-Handed World – for Teachers and Parents of Left-handed Children

By Diane Paul, The Robinswood Press, Stourbridge, 1998, 2002, 2008, (BMA Highly Commended), £11.95.

The Optimum Nutrition Cookbook
By Patrick Holford and Judy Ridgway, Piatkus, London, 2010, £14.99.

Optimum Nutrition for Your Child's Mind
By Patrick Holford and Deborah Colson, Piatkus Books, London, 2006, £10.99.

Ritalin Free Kids: Homeopathic Medicine for ADHD and Other Behavioral and Learning Problems
By Judyth Reichenberg-Ullman and Robert Ullman, Prima, USA, 1997. 2nd edition, 2000, £7.68.

Scattered: How Attention Deficit Disorder Originates and What You Can Do About It
By Dr Gabor Mate, Plume Books, 2000, £9.00.

Special Educational Needs – A Parent's Guide
By Antonia Chitty and Victoria Dawson, Need2Know, Peterborough, 2008, £8.99.

Socially ADDept: A Manual for Parents of Children with ADHD and/or Learning Disabilities
By Janet Z Giler, PhD, CES Continuing Education Seminars, 2000, £28.14.

The Churkendoose Anthology: True Stories of Triumph over Neurological Dysfunction
By Judith Bluestone, The HANDLE Institute, www.handle.org. 2002. (Amazon) £144.70. Used £8.51.

The Fabric of Autism, Weaving The Threads Into A Cogent Theory
By Judith Bluestone, Lewis County Historical Society or The HANDLE Institute, www.handle.org, 2007, £17.50.

The Gluten Free Cookbook,
Kyle Cathie, 2006, £4.99

The Gluten Free Cookbook for Kids,
By Adriana Rabinovich, Vermilion 2009, £12.00

They Are What You Feed Them: How Food Can Improve Your Child's Behaviour, Learning and Mood
By Dr Alex Richardson, Harper Thorsons, London, 2010, £12.99.

Understanding ADHD – A Parent's Guide to Attention Deficit Hyperactivity Disorder in Children
By Christopher Green and Kit Chee, Vermilion, London, 2nd Rev Ed, 1997, £9.99.

Understanding your hyperactive child: the essential guide for parents
By Eric A Taylor, Vermilion, London, 1997.

Vegetarian Cooking Without: Recipes free from added sugar, yeast, dairy products, meat, fish, saturated fat
By Barbara Cousins, Thorsons, London, 2000, £10.99.

Victory Over ADHD, A holistic approach for helping children with Attention Deficit Hyperactivity Disorder
By Deborah Merlin & Larry Cook, Book Publishing Company, 2009, £12.50

Why Your Child is Hyperactive
By Ben F Feingold, Random House, USA, 1985, 1988 Edition, £7.46.

Need2Know

Need - 2 - Know

Available Titles Include ...

Allergies A Parent's Guide
ISBN 978-1-86144-064-8 £8.99

Autism A Parent's Guide
ISBN 978-1-86144-069-3 £8.99

Blood Pressure The Essential Guide
ISBN 978-1-86144-067-9 £8.99

Dyslexia and Other Learning Difficulties
A Parent's Guide ISBN 978-1-86144-042-6 £8.99

Bullying A Parent's Guide
ISBN 978-1-86144-044-0 £8.99

Epilepsy The Essential Guide
ISBN 978-1-86144-063-1 £8.99

Your First Pregnancy The Essential Guide
ISBN 978-1-86144-066-2 £8.99

Gap Years The Essential Guide
ISBN 978-1-86144-079-2 £8.99

Secondary School A Parent's Guide
ISBN 978-1-86144-093-8 £9.99

Primary School A Parent's Guide
ISBN 978-1-86144-088-4 £9.99

Applying to University The Essential Guide
ISBN 978-1-86144-052-5 £8.99

ADHD The Essential Guide
ISBN 978-1-86144-060-0 £8.99

Student Cookbook – Healthy Eating The Essential Guide
ISBN 978-1-86144-069-3 £8.99

Multiple Sclerosis The Essential Guide
ISBN 978-1-86144-086-0 £8.99

Coeliac Disease The Essential Guide
ISBN 978-1-86144-087-7 £9.99

Special Educational Needs A Parent's Guide
ISBN 978-1-86144-116-4 £9.99

The Pill An Essential Guide
ISBN 978-1-86144-058-7 £8.99

University A Survival Guide
ISBN 978-1-86144-072-3 £8.99

View the full range at **www.need2knowbooks.co.uk**.
To order our titles call **01733 898103**, email **sales@ n2kbooks.com** or visit the website. Selected ebooks available online.

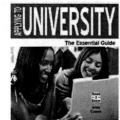
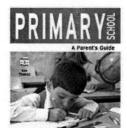

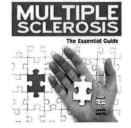

Need - 2 - Know, Remus House, Coltsfoot Drive, Peterborough, PE2 9BF